CONTAINER CONJURE

Crafting Magic with Jars, Bottles, Bags & More

STARR CASAS

Foreword by Cory Thomas Hutcheson

WEISER BOOKS

This edition first published in 2026 by Weiser Books, an imprint of
Red Wheel/Weiser, LLC
With offices at:
65 Parker Street, Suite 7
Newburyport, MA 01950
www.redwheelweiser.com

ISBN: 978-1-57863-889-5

Library of Congress Cataloging-in-Publication Data available on request.
Cover photographs © Starr Casas
Cover and interior design by Sky Peck Design
Interior images from iStock.com and Sky Peck Design
Typeset in Adobe Jenson Pro

Printed in the United States of America
IBI
10 9 8 7 6 5 4 3 2 1

MIX
Paper
FSC® C183721

This book is dedicated to
all the Big Mamas, past, present, and future!
To all Conjure workers—keep it real!

Warning

Any reader who uses the work within this book does so entirely at their own risk! The author and publisher accept no liability if the spells do not have the desired effect or if adverse effects are caused.

This book is not suitable for children.

CONTENTS

FOREWORD

One of the best things about being a folklorist is the people you get to know. In the best cases, you get to spend many hours with the people known as "tradition-bearers," those who contain and carry the history and practices of their culture with them. Sometimes you get to talk to a person for only a little while, even as you feel them brimming with stories, wisdom, knowledge, and discernment, and it breaks your heart that you have such a short time with them. If you're very lucky, you get brought into the orbit of these folks more than once, and you begin to see and feel the richness of the world that lives within them, and you can start to see how a person can hold entire communities and histories wound around their very bones.

Starr Casas is one of those people for me. I've had the good fortune to meet her in person only once at a magical conference in New Orleans, but it was an experience that has stuck with me for years. It was less about what she was teaching (a discussion of the Walls of Jericho and reversal magic, if memory serves) and more about the fact that she was a natural center of gravity for old school magical workers from all walks of life. She conversed with Wiccan practitioners and Trad Craft witches, sure, but she seemed always most at home with the people who had grown up in the Southern soil soaked with magic. She talked openly of saints and hex work, parlayed with a Gullah woman about traditions from the Georgia Sea Islands, and knew how to get a whole crowd of people up and moving to feel the magic that ran in their bodies and blood. Getting to see Starr in action was a gift, one that I'm thankful for in my time on this earth. I have also been lucky enough to work with her on other projects, including acting as her editor for a chapter in a book on North American folk magic. She is always completely genuine in her writing, and that same easy, at-home feeling I got when interacting with her at that conference all those years ago translates directly onto the page.

I have said before and I will never stop saying that the pleasure of reading one of Starr's books is that you have a seat at her kitchen table. What she shares through her writing is valuable for the information and wisdom she's spent a lifetime accumulating, and that's absolutely one of the reasons to turn the following pages. Even more than the bare bones information on what sorts of containers can hold which kinds of work or which tools are most useful for doing a divination to see if a work is warranted, though, are her stories.

Starr draws stories from her life to illustrate each of her works, putting them in context in a way that lets you truly *feel* how the work happens in the real world. She'll tell you about her daughter confronting a hotfoot jinx and why keeping some ammonia on hand is helpful for both physical *and* spiritual cleaning. She'll introduce you to Miss Sallie Mae and show you how thinking through a working—knowing if it is justified and how to deal with the aftermath—is something to do before you unscrew the lid of the old jelly jar you're about to pop someone's name into.

Reading Starr's stories is entering the world of Conjure and container work from a place of rooted practice and everyday living, and you walk away with more than just theories and a grocery list of ingredients. Instead, when you finish this book, I believe that you will feel like you've been a guest in Starr's home, helped her load up a few packets and jars, and that you will feel comfortable taking your own practice with container Conjure into the real world. You won't be afraid to get a little dirty, a little messy, and a lot magical.

Container work by its nature is all of those: dirty, messy, and magical. There's something about slipping someone's name paper into a jar of honey and getting your fingers coated with the sticky, amber nectar and then licking them clean that turns magic into something visceral. Jars are only one kind of container, though, and one of the joys of the pages ahead will be the way that Starr gets you to see just about anything as a potential container: a dried gourd from your garden, a fallen bird's nest, or an apple on your kitchen counter.

You use what you have on hand, the way that our ancestors did, and the magic follows suit and takes the shape of the container you give it. Starr guides you to understand the traditions and very much draws upon the lessons she's learned over a lifetime of Conjure, but she also makes it abundantly clear that you are a magical container yourself, and your powers of enchantment are limited only by your imagination. If that's not a reason to pull up a metaphorical seat at her table, I don't know what is.

I hope that you will spend some time with Starr here and get to know container magic a little better. More importantly, I hope you will get to know her better and find your life more magical for it. I think you will.

—Cory Thomas Hutcheson,
author of *New World Witchery* and editor of
Llewellyn's Complete Book of North American Folk Magic

INTRODUCTION

Container works are some of the oldest works around. A container is simply something that a work can be placed in. It could be many different things that can hold the work. This can be a jar, a dollie, a dirt dauber's nest (dirt daubers are a type of wasp whose nests are found on porches). A Conjure bag or a Conjure packet is a container that holds the roots and herbs and the petition of the work within it. It is a container even if it is made out of cloth. Dolls are sewn and then stuffed with roots and herbs and petitions; personal concerns are also added to them for the work, which makes them a container.

Container work is not new to older workers. Jar works are a new way to work. I started working with them about thirty-five years ago. The ingredients that are placed in them are not new; it's simply the use of the jar that is a new concept. Back in the old days, the elders wouldn't have used a jar for doing work because jars were used to can their food or to keep the food safe from rodents and things. They wouldn't have wasted a jar on work. In today's world, we throw empty jars away most of the time, so they are very useful to hold work. I've always worked with them, but I didn't offer them to clients until two of my clients hotfooted themselves from their own homes using my hotfoot powder to get rid of two separate neighbors. One sold her home and the other one left her home for about a year. They wanted to do the work themselves instead of letting me do it, so I decided that it was better to sell containers that hold the ingredients than to sell the powder and let them do the work themselves.

The other thing about container jars is you can shake the jar to keep the work moving and working. If you just let it sit there, the power of the work will stop working. All work has to be worked and fed in order to keep the work moving.

Some of this work can be dangerous and shouldn't be taken lightly, like hotfoot powder. Hotfoot is worked with to remove someone from your home, a job, or a situation, to get them out of the way. Not only is it the type of work that should be contained, but also you must use discernment before doing it. I will talk about hotfoot work later on in these pages, but I need to stress that it is not the type of work that you take lightly. Some folks believe that you can drop hotfoot work and it will only affect the person that it is intended for; my experience tells me that anybody who gets in that powder or oil is going to be affected by it, so container work is the best work for this type of magic. Each worker has to do whatever they feel is best for them. Just remember that it can't be taken lightly; use discernment with this work.

One time I made a hotfoot powder for another worker. She had a job that someone had hired her to do at the time when I made the powder for her. I did not know that the target worked at the same place my daughter worked. So, I'm here at home, minding my own business, and my daughter calls me. She said, "Mama, I think somebody is trying to hotfoot me out of my job." She said, "I was fine when

I came to work, but I went outside and when I came back in, my feet started burning and I started getting really aggravated." So I knew that that was hotfoot.

My daughter told me that she immediately went and cleaned her shoes off with ammonia and cleaned her hands real good and she started to feel better. I told her that I would call her back in a few minutes. So I called the worker that I had given the hotfoot to and sure enough that hotfoot powder was sprinkled where my daughter worked. The target worked there, so I called my daughter back and I told her what had happened. During that time they lost quite a few employees.

Now, the worker that I sold that powder to said that she put the target's picture and their name burned to ash and added them into the powder. Well, apparently it didn't work the way she thought it was gonna work. So, when you're doing this type of work you have to use discernment. You have to make sure that the way you're laying the trick down is the best way to lay it down, and in an instance like this a container work would have been the right work to do.

Container work is, in my opinion, the best work to do when you are doing long-term magic. Once again, this is what I have learned from experience. If you let a work just sit there, eventually the magic is going to run out. In order for a work to be successful, you have to feed that work; you have to keep that work moving. Not all magic is long-term and ongoing. It depends on the type of job that you are doing, and ther are many different ways to do magic or Conjure. Sometimes, though, a job will take longer to do, and in those times, hey, container work is the best way to go. So, if you were trying to nail someone or something down, then you would not work that work like you would if you were trying to draw something to you.

When you do a container jar, for instance, you put that jar together and then that jar is shaken three times a day to draw whatever you are trying to draw to you, or to move someone that you are trying to move away from you. If you were trying to nail someone down, a jar work would not be my first choice when working the magic. When you nail someone down it means you are literally stopping them to keep them from moving, just like if you nail something to the wall.

In this book, you will find many different ways to do container magic. The only thing that's gonna stop you is your imagination and yourself. If it's a container, it can be worked with. If it can be *made* into a container, it can be worked with. Some of these works are very old and not talked about anymore. You have to remember that Conjure workers don't have any threefold law and such to govern us; if the work is justified, then it is okay to do. You find out whether the work is justified by throwing the bones, reading cards, or some other form of divination. Discernment is a big thing in Conjure.

I hope that everyone can learn something from this book.

DISCERNMENT

Discernment is a big part, or it *should* be a big part, of any type of magical work. You have to be able to know if you should be doing a type of work or not, and the only way to find this out is to be able to understand what spirit is telling you.

Discernment and confusion go hand in hand. When we are upset, we cannot think straight, which makes us confused, and when we are confused we lose the gift of discernment. Being able to see what is really going on underneath the surface, not just what is in front of your face, all the confusion, drama, and trauma, is a gift; it's called the gift of discernment. In order to be able to see what is truly going on, you have to be able to become calm and get your emotions under control. You cannot let them control you. Sometimes this is not an easy thing to do, and it takes practice. You need to have patience because you have to be in total control of your emotions. When I am upset, I stop and take three deep breaths slowly; I have found that this helps me get centered and then I can think. I then sit down in a quiet place with a candle and a clean, clear glass of water and just watch that candle flame. It seems to settle my mind and helps me to relax so I can truly focus on all the answers that I am trying to find.

Some folks are born with the gift of discernment and need no tools. Spirit speaks strongly to them. Others, I have found, have to learn how to discern what is going on in a situation. They may do this by working with some type of tool that helps them to see the whole situation, and it may even show them how to fix the issue. If you find yourself not understanding what the spirit is trying to tell you through laying out the tarot cards or playing cards, or maybe throwing the bones, then you need to have some other type of divination tool so that you can understand what the spirit is trying to tell you.

A pendulum would be a good way to get yes or no answers. I train all my pendulums to move for yes and stop for no, because all that round in a circle and back and forth is so confusing to me that by the time I finally get the answer I'm frustrated and aggravated trying to figure out what that pendulum was trying to tell me. So to keep it simple, like this work is, I trained my pendulums.

If you don't like working with a pendulum, then you can either make a set of three charms out of clay or you can get three bones to work with. They have clay nowadays that gets hard on its own; you don't have to bake it. You simply take your clay and work it into three round discs. The disc needs to be about the size of a half dollar. Once you make the shape of the disc, you need to take a nail. On one side of each disc write the word "yes," and on the other side write the word "no." Let the discs dry, then you can paint them if you want to. If you are going to be working with three bones, then you write "yes" on one side of all three and "no" on the other side. Now you have a divination tool that will be easy to understand.

The next step is to dedicate the tool to a spirit so the spirit can help you find the information you are looking for. Saint Lucy and

Saint Claire are two good saints to work with. They are both saints of clarity that I work with when I want to see a situation. Some say Saint Lucy was a Pagan. Below is the prayer I work with for Saint Lucy, and I will also give you the instructions on how to empower the tool.

Before you start the dedication, you should say three Our Fathers, three Hail Marys, and three Apostles' Creeds.

Blessed Saint Lucy, I petition you to fill these bones with your gift of sight so that I may obtain perfect vision and discernment when I throw them. I petition you to help my mind understand what my eyes are seeing Holy Mother, let me understand all that I see. In your holy name I pray.

If you decide to do this dedication, you will need to do it at least three days in a row. Nine days in a row would be best. You need a white handkerchief to lay the bones on and you need four white vigil candles. Lay the tools down on the white handkerchief, then place one white candle at the top, one white candle at the bottom, one white candle to the left, and one white candle to the right. You then light the first candle that you laid down and say the prayer to Saint Lucy. Then you go to the next candle that you sat down and you say the prayer again. You repeat the process until all the candles are lit. You need to say the prayer over your divination tool three times. Then you leave the candles burning. (Remember to practice fire safety.) You will repeat your prayers three times a day for either the three or nine days. Once the prayers are done, you can tie your divination tool up in the white handkerchief and take the bones out as needed.

Every time that you work with your divination tools, you should have a glass of water and a white candle dedicated to Saint Lucy.

Before you throw, you need to say three Our Fathers, three Hail Marys, and three Apostles' Creeds. Then you say your petition to Saint Lucy that she may help you to see everything that you need to see in the situation, and to tell you if you should even be doing the work at all. After that you throw the bones and see what comes up. Of course, if you get three "no," then that means no! A definite no! If you get three "yes," then that is a strong yes, and you can move on and do the work.

Sometimes it's not that plain, so I have always made it a habit that if I get more of one answer than I do the other, then that's my answer. For instance, if I throw and I get two "no" and one "yes," I have come to understand that it can be done, but I'm probably gonna have issues or that I need to change the work. If I get two "yes" and one "no," then I take it to mean that I can do the work but it may take longer than what I thought. When that happens, I usually will ask if I can do something extra to boost the work to make it move at a good pace.

It all depends on what the work is and what I feel when I am asking permission to do the work. Magic is not black and white. There are a lot of shadow spaces within it. Sometimes spirit doesn't give us all the answers that we're looking for. That is when our own discernment comes into play and we have to have good judgment. Not only do we have to listen to our feelings, but also we have to hear what spirit is telling us. We all have that little voice in our mind and sometimes it instantly says, "No, don't do it." At those times I have learned that, no matter how I feel about a situation, I have to leave it alone because I know if I don't it's probably not gonna turn out the way I think it should.

So just take your time. Go slow. Practice throwing your bones or working with your pendulum or even throwing out three tarot or playing cards. Most importantly, you have to learn to listen to what the spirits that walk with you are trying to tell you.

It takes practice and skill, but I feel like everyone has this gift, and some just don't know how to bring the gift forward. This is one of the reasons I wanted to talk about this in this book. I'm not sure that you can teach someone how to listen to the spirit of discernment, but I'm going to try here.

If you look in the Bible, you will see passages where it talks about discernment and being able to see what is going on in a situation. If you open the Bible and look at Ephesians 5 V 6–10, it tells us not to be deceived by empty words. In other places in the Bible, it warns us to look deeper, for us not to let our eyes fool us with what we see on the outside, but to discern what is really on the inside.

> 6 Let no one deceive you with empty words, for because of these things the wrath of God comes upon the sons of disobedience. 7 Therefore do not become partners with them; 8 for at one time you were darkness, but now you are light in the Lord. Walk as children of light (9 for the fruit of light is found in all that is good and right and true), 10 and try to discern what is pleasing to the Lord.

Sometimes God, or the Holy Spirit, whatever you choose to call the higher power, tries to warn us and show us how to move around some folks. They give us these feelings that we feel inside around some people that let us know that we should not be dealing with them folks. Most of the time, we try to look at the good parts of a person instead of looking at the *whole* person. We will ignore those warnings and try to build a bond with someone that the Holy Spirit has warned us against. We don't listen either because we think we know more than the Holy Spirit does, or because we don't know how to discern what the Holy Spirit is trying to tell us. When we do this, nine times out of ten, we regret it later on. It could be years before that person shows you their true colors or it could be almost instantly, but either way, if we would have just listened to what spirit was trying to tell us, then we would not have gotten our hearts broken. We would not have been in the middle of a bunch of trauma and drama. That's why it's so important to learn to discern and to listen to what the Holy Spirit is telling you. For me, every time I don't listen to spirit I live to regret it! In those times, I don't have anybody else to blame but myself. Spirit showed me what was going on and I chose to ignore it and follow what I wanted to do instead.

When we choose not to listen to that inner voice, those feelings that we get around some folks, then we cannot blame anybody but ourselves.

One thing is for sure: When you do not use discernment in those times, those lessons that you learn hurt, and they usually break your heart. They are usually lessons that you will never forget in your life, because you did not listen to the Holy Spirit and you did not use the gifts that they gave you to remove yourself from that situation before it ever started. You did what you thought was best instead. That's why it's so important to listen and to understand discernment and how the Holy Spirit talks to you when they are trying to guide you in the direction that you need to go.

Prayers for Discernment

Philippians 1 V 9

And this I pray, that your love may abound still more and more in knowledge and all discernment.

Isaiah 11 V 2–3

2 The Spirit of the Lord shall rest upon Him,
The Spirit of wisdom and understanding,
The Spirit of counsel and might,
The Spirit of knowledge and of the fear of the Lord.

3 His delight is in the fear of the Lord,
And He shall not judge by the sight of His eyes,
Nor decide by the hearing of His ears.

WHAT IS CONTAINER WORK?

The first thing to remember is when you work magic you are causing energy to shift. You have to remember that energy is neither good nor bad. It simply moves. Conjure work is the type of work that either draws something in, holds it down, or removes it out of the way. There are many different categories of work. It doesn't matter if you are doing the work in a container or some other type of work. For this book, we are only looking at container works. You will find the different types of container works in the next section of the book called Container Categories, but I want to make sure you understand different types of container works before we move on so you will better understand them when you try to put your works together.

For example, Miss Sally Mae has been having issues with her husband. For the last six months, they have been fighting like cats and dogs ever since he lost his job at the beginning of the year. Now the situation has reached a boiling point. Sally Mae's husband has walked out. Once he left the home, she found out that he had been fooling around with another woman. The gossip in the streets says this other woman may have had a hand in her husband leaving. Miss Sally Mae is looking for something to help her get him back in the house where he belongs.

Q: What should she do and how should Miss Sally Mae work this job? What categories does this situation fall under?

A: This situation falls under all of the categories (see page 19). The first step is to do a cleansing so she can remove whatever it is that has moved her husband out of the house and is causing all these issues.

This is why cleansing work should be the first thing you do in this type of situation. Sally Mae let the situation get out of hand. It has gotten to the point where he walked out, so now she has to cool things off. You can't think with a hot head. Cooling his head will make it easier to get him to do what she wants. That's the first part of the work, which is cleansing and healing.

Now for the second part, you have to take control of the situation. It's time for Sally Mae to get control of her man. Since it has already gone too far, she needs to start with some domination work. I was taught and I believe that anytime you try to dominate a target, you need to add a little confusion into the work, and a little lavender to soothe their nerves so they don't realize that they are being worked on. This is why it's important to make sure your target has a cool head. Hotheadedness and confusion don't mix well together.

In addition to doing domination work, Miss Sally needs to add drawing and sweetening to the work so she can get her man back where he belongs.

Once she gets his behind home where he belongs and gets things settled down, then it is time to deal with the old hussy who dared to break up a happy home. It's time for some souring work. This needs to be done to sour the relationship with the other woman so he won't be tempted to step out again. Slow it down to a halt! You can use vinegar because it sours, but molasses is another good ingredient because it pours slowly, and anything that pours slowly is going to move slowly.

I know molasses is sweet, so you may be thinking, "How is it not gonna sweeten his and the other woman's relationship?" The reason is this is Conjure work, not some other type of magical working, and in Conjure we are taught that if it pours slowly then it will work slowly! I know molasses is given to some saints as offerings, like Saint Martha the Dominator, and in those cases it is not to slow things down but to get things moving, so it may seem contradictory. I can't explain how or why it works differently, I can only say from experience that it does! Maybe it is a combination of the other ingredients and the prayers. I don't know, but I do know it works. If you make a molasses jar, not only will it put a stop to all that running around but it will also slow down the affection that he feels for the other woman.

Miss Sally Mae and her man started having problems when he lost his job. Now it's time for her to do some money work to draw some money back into the home and to get a job with a good income for her husband so he won't have so much time on his hands. Like the old folks say: Idle hands are the devil's workshop. It's not good for men to have too much time on their hands. Men need to feel useful; they need to feel like they are taking care of the home and the family. When they feel they are not providing as they should, or they feel they are not wanted and loved enough, they will look elsewhere. There is always someone waiting on the sidelines to take your place. This is the third part of the working on the situation. This would make this work a triple-action work, because you are doing three different types of work on the same situation. Always remember: It may take more than one work to get a job done because there is usually more than one element in the mix causing the issue. You have to look at the job from every angle in order to really see exactly what types of work need to be done to reach success. It may seem like a lot of work, and it is, but in the long run you benefit from it and your life is a lot better and runs a lot smoother.

In this situation, this is where we do the nailing down and protection work we feel that job needs. This is the fourth and final part of the work. Sally Mae's prayers and hard work have brought her husband back home. It has eliminated the problem for now, but if she wants to keep love and happiness in her home with her husband, she is going to have to nail down the situation. She needs to nail her husband down so he won't run around in the streets anymore, looking for what he feels he is lacking at home, and she needs to nail his job down so he will always have a stable income flowing into her home. Then you cover all of this work with protection work to make sure that your home and your husband are well protected. Sally Mae also needs to go as far as nailing the other woman down so that she cannot come back and start messing with her husband again. If she doesn't take care of that situation, it's a possibility that it will rear its head up again, and next time it may be harder to get rid of the other woman.

When you have a sticky situation, you can't just throw something together and expect it to magically take care of what is going on. It takes work, lots of work. This is where the saying goes: "If it's something that you have to fight too hard for, and it keeps reoccurring, it might not be the right thing for you." To achieve total success for yourself, or to help others, you have to do what it takes to get the job done.

Most of the time this requires doing more than one job at a time and hitting the target from different angles until you see results.

Sometimes it may even take a while before you see results. You have to understand that, just as bad as you want something to happen, the target likes their life. They wanna keep doing what they're doing. It becomes a battle of wills, and it all comes down to who has the strongest will and the strongest determination. That's who wins in the end.

If it seems like the work or works you are doing are not getting you anywhere, then you need to do a reading on the situation. This is because you may want to revamp what you are doing or change the work up completely. You have to remember that this work is not one-size-fits-all. What worked on one target might not work on another one. The first target might not have had a strong will, while the second target may dig in and, as hard as you're trying to force them to do your will, they are battling it. So therefore you may have to change up the work that you are doing.

Something that an elder told me is if a target knows you and they know how you work, it makes it easy for them to block your work or for them to undo your work. In those instances, you need to do a type of work that they don't know that you know how to do. So if your target is a Conjure worker, and you're a Conjure worker, then you might want to change it up and do some other type of spiritual work where they don't have a clue that you know what you're doing. If you don't know anything else, then ask someone to help you with some advice on some other types of magic.

Magic is always gonna take the road of least resistance so be wise in your workings. If you are doing a magical work and it seems like nothing is going the way it is supposed to, then you probably need to do a reading on what you are doing because the work is going to take the easiest route. This happens sometimes when we do not listen to what the Holy Spirit is trying to tell us and we don't use our gifts to discern what is the best route to take. Sometimes the simplest works are the best works. They will sometimes get the job done faster than a long, drawn-out working. It is very important that you always check with spirit first; remember, the only rule to Conjure work is that the work be justified. If it is justified work, you are safe, but if you work on someone and it is unjustified, you take a chance of getting hit with your own work.

Just be very mindful of the work you do because you are the only one responsible for your actions. Remember this always: Just because you know how to do something, it doesn't mean you should! In Conjure, justification is everything.

CONTAINER CATEGORIES

A container is anything that a work can be loaded into. There are many different containers, some even animal parts. A container work is not much different than any other magical work you might do. The difference is that this type of work is contained in a certain type of vessel. This could be a bowl, a lamp, a crawfish pincher, a crab shell, even a beef tongue. It all depends on why you are doing the work.

Even though this work is simple and basic, it is very powerful if it is done right. In my experience, you don't need a bunch of supplies and a lot of hocus-pocus to make magic happen. In this section, I want to talk about the different types of work that can be done in the different types of containers.

When I was growing up, my auntie sewed clothes for a living. I remember she had two different pincushions that she used to hold her pins. One of them was just a pincushion covered with material and stuffed; the other one was kind of dressy and had a cute little lace doily covering it. The first was full of stick pins, but the cute little lace one had only a few pins in it. I could play with the one that was full of stick pins, but she didn't want me messing with the lace one, even though every once in a while I got to play with it. I loved it because it was so pretty. I found out years later that a pincushion with a dollie on top of it can be worked with to hold someone down. My uncle was a hot damn mess, so I'm pretty sure that he was under that lace somewhere.

Even a photo can become a container if it is worked with to hold the ingredients of the work. There is a simple Shut Your Mouth work that works wonderfully with a photo of a target. You need

a marker
a photo of the target
a little glue
red thread
a penny

The photo becomes a packet. Draw a circle around the target's head in the photo, and place an X over each of the eyes and three Xs across the mouth. Then you make a cross over the face. Next, you place a little glue on the back of the penny and you petition Saint Ramon to shut the target's mouth. Place the penny over the three Xs over the mouth and let it dry. Once the penny is glued to the photo, you fold the photo into a small packet around the penny. Take some red thread and bind the packet closed. You can then place the little packet in the freezer, or you can place it in some sugar water in a zipper bag and then place that in the freezer if you are trying to sweeten the target's mouth toward you. This is a very effective way to stop someone who loves to gossip and drag folks' names around.

Drawing

Drawing covers a lot of areas in Conjure work. Some of these areas include steady work, reconciliation, love, money, success, peace, prosperity, and better business, just to name a few and give you an idea of what this type of work covers. Drawing work is a very popular type of work. Folks work with this type of magic to keep their money flowing, to keep their job going, and to bring new things into their life.

I want to give you an example of how drawing magic works. There are as many different works that can be done as there are workers; no two workers will ever work the same. They may be similar, but will never be the same, because no two workers have the same sauce.

When you're doing magic to draw something to you, you need something that pulls; this can be a lodestone, which is a naturally magnetized rock, or you can work with a magnet. I prefer to work with a magnet when I'm trying to draw something in because the magnet has a stronger pull. If you are trying to draw in more money, for example, then you take the largest bill that you have in your wallet and place it between two magnets.

You have to remember that like begets like. I don't ever work with fake money or what some folks call spirit money. I was taught to use real money because I am trying to draw real money into my life, not pretty money to look at. I want to be able to use the money to pay bills and such.

I like working with blue candles to draw in money. You can take the money that you have put between the two magnets, which is a money packet in its own right, bind it to a glass vigil candle, and then burn the candle daily while saying your prayer and petition over the candle. Once the candle burns out, you can take the money with the magnets still attached to it and place it in your wallet. This way the packet can continue to draw money into your wallet.

This may seem like simple magic but I have found that it works very well. Once a month you simply take the packet out of your wallet and bind it on another candle. The color of the candle is your choice. Like I said, I prefer blue wax for money, but you can use whatever color you like to feed the money and the magnets. Then you put the packet right back in your wallet and let it continue to do its job.

Removing

Removing work covers reversal work, cleansing, blockbuster cut and clear types of work, such as hotfoot, and any other types of work that you do to remove a situation out of your way. These works are part of the foundation of Conjure. There are times when a situation comes up that has to be taken care of. If you have blocks in your life where nothing you do is working, then you have to do what I call a blockbuster to remove all those blocks out of your way. If you feel like you are justified and someone has jinxed you or crossed you up, that is when you need to do reversal work.

This work removes the jinx or cross condition off of you and sends it back where it came from. Energy will always go back where it came from if the work is done right. Spirit always knows where the energies came from. You don't have to tell them; they already know. You simply have to do the work.

Magic is energy and it goes where it is directed, so therefore if someone can direct negative energy to you, you can reverse it and send it right back where it came from. When doing this type of reversal work, I was taught not to ever call out names, even though I may know good and well who is doing the work against me. This is because I might not see everything and I might miss something or miss a target, or I could even hit the wrong person. So when doing reversal work, I suggest that you just say, "I return all crossed conditions back to where they came from, to all enemies known and unknown," and send it back to the source that it came from. This way you don't hit the wrong person, and the right person is going to get exactly what they sent out plus some extra. Also, never put a limit on spirit. Just ask them to do the reversal and let them hand out the justice as they see fit.

Love

Love work covers all areas of love. I have found through the experience of doing this work professionally for over forty-plus years that a lot of folks come looking for magic work to bring someone back into their life, draw someone to them, or make someone love them. The thing is, in order to find true love, you have to first love yourself.

You will hear me say this a few times within this book but like begets like. If you don't have good self-esteem or confidence within yourself, you are going to draw one of two different types of people. You will either draw someone who has the same issues that you have, or you will draw someone who sees themselves as being the power behind the relationship. This type of person will probably take control and walk all over you.

Self-love should be at the top of your list of love works to start with. When you love yourself, you are not prone to settle; you're not looking for someone to make you a better person. You know you're a better person because you know you are a powerful person. You don't need just anyone; you want someone to be a partner in life and you stand on it. This will make you examine folks better and you won't just settle for someone because they fill a missing place in your life.

When we love ourselves, it changes the whole way that we look at love and at being loved. Does this mean that you will never need to do magic to draw someone back into your life who may have left? No. Does this mean that you will never have to do love work to draw someone new into your life? It absolutely does not. But it does mean that the things that you are looking for within a person change. You will not settle. You will no longer be looking for someone to validate you, you will be looking for them for companionship, someone to share your life with. It's not that you have to have them. You're perfectly fine alone, but you prefer *not* to be alone.

When you love yourself, it changes your whole perspective on life. It also changes how folks treat you, how you allow them to treat you, and also how you look at yourself. Love of self makes life a lot easier and much more enjoyable.

Money

I have found that money work, like love work, covers a broader area of magic. Money work covers everything dealing with money, from finding a job to making someone pay you money that they owe you. In my experience, and as I have dealt with, money work and love work are the two most sought-after works in magic. The old folks used to say that money is the root of all evil. I don't believe this to be true. I believe instead that man does evil for the love of money. When I was growing up, my mama raised us to believe that as long as you had everything that you needed to survive then you were rich. She never put a strong emphasis on money; it was the complete opposite. So when I started doing money work as a young worker I had to change my whole way of thinking because of the way I was raised.

Even today, I have folks come to me for help with prosperity. They're worried about getting the money they're asking for because of something going wrong somewhere else with someone they love. I used to think like that; I don't anymore. We have to change the way we look at money and how we feel about doing money magic. We have to remember that what is for us is gonna be for *us*, and it's there just waiting for us to ask for it.

I had someone tell me one time if it's there waiting for me, then why hasn't the Holy Spirit given it to me? Spirit cannot just step in on your behalf; they have to be invited in. Everything costs something; nothing is for free. You have to do the work and you have to be consistent. You have to know that you deserve everything that you want and everything that you need. You can't petition spirit to bring you money and prosperity then lounge around the house in your underwear all day, waiting for it to drop in your hands. It doesn't work that way!

You have to do the work, then you have to make money, and keep it going. You cannot just light a few candles one time and expect money to start flowing in, or that you're gonna become rich immediately. It *could* happen, but I've not seen it happen yet. The ideal money work is that you keep a steady flow of cash coming in. If you spend twenty-five dollars somewhere down the road, you get that twenty-five dollars back plus extra. If you have a steady flow of cash, then your money work is a success.

You have to be reasonable; you have to set a goal and stick with it. You have to focus on one amount at a time. If you have a bill you need to pay, put it in a can and feed that can change every day. Claim that that bill is paid and, before you know it, that money is going to get to you so you can pay that bill.

Where spirit is concerned, you have to be very positive. You cannot say things like, *oh, I'm broke all the time, nothing never goes right, everything I touch turns to crap*. You cannot claim those types of negative energies. You should never use negative words when it comes to yourself, because if you say it enough, spirit is going to begin to believe it. Then the car's gonna break down, then other things are gonna start happening that cost money, and you really are gonna be in a bad financial situation.

When my husband and I first got married, he was a worrier. He worried about money. We didn't have a lot of money, and he worried about it all the time, and then one day my mama told him, "The more you worry about money, the less you are going to have because you're telling God that you don't believe that he will provide for you. You have to change the way you think about money and the way you deal with money. Once you get everything lined up, you should see a steady flow of cash."

You also cannot worry about where the money is coming from. You simply do the work and the money will find its way to you. It could be through someone who owes you money that you forgot they owed you. The spirits that walk with you will always take care of you. You simply have to do the work and have the faith that the things that you need are gonna be given to you. Discernment plays a big part in this. You should always check and see if the work you're doing is working and if what you're asking for is gonna be a success. If you get a "no," then change the petition up until you get a "yes," and remember that you deserve to have your dreams come true. Magic opens the door to help make that happen.

Protection

Spiritual protection work should be kept up and ongoing. It is a very important part of keeping yourself and your family spiritually protected. In these magical streets, not everyone is going to love you and not everyone is going to have your best interest in their hearts. I have found over the years of dealing with spiritual folks that there is a lot of envy and jealousy out there. Does that mean that you are constantly being jinxed and crossed? No, it doesn't. Every issue you have in your life doesn't necessarily have to do with magic being thrown at you. But if someone studies you enough with negative thoughts and feelings toward you, remember, thoughts are energy. When you focus on someone long enough, those energies can hit a target. For magic to hit, there has to be focus, and if someone is studying you or they are focused on your downfall, it will eventually start to cause issues. You have to remember that words and thoughts are very powerful.

You never know really how some folks truly feel about you because they can hide it so well. You may feel like they're your best friend, that they love you to death, and that they truly care about you, when the truth is, inside, their heart is filled with envy and jealousy. It's always better to keep your guard up and keep your home and your family well protected than to let your guard down and let things start going wrong within your home and your life.

You may think, "Well, I don't have anything for anybody to be jealous of. Most of my friends have more than me." I have found that it doesn't matter *what* they have—they just don't want *you* to have what you've got. I know that sounds weird, but this is what I have seen dealing with folks that have been in my life for thirty or forty years who I had thought were our friends. So protection work is a very important part of this work, along with cleansing and reversal. You have to pay attention to actions more than you do words. Like my mama used to say, "A pair of lips can say anything but those actions never lie."

I had someone tell me that I don't trust folks because I haven't dealt with past trauma; it's because of those past traumas I want to see what folks do and not what they say. When I'm told that, it makes me look at these folks differently because then I begin to wonder, why do they want me to let my guard down? What are they really after? What's in it for them? Why do they want me to share my inner feelings with them? Why do they even care?

It has nothing to do with trauma, except for the lessons I have learned in life that folks have shown me. I have very strong boundaries when it comes to my personal business. If you are digging in my life and my business, I'mma slam that door shut! You have to be careful how much you let folks know about your habits and the way you live your life, because it could make you an easy target should a friend turn into a friend-enemy or maybe just a plain ol' enemy! Don't let folks get too close, lest they know your weaknesses. Keep those protections up and keep them strong!

Domination

Domination work covers all works where you need to have the upper hand. For me, this comes in all different strengths. Some are stronger than others; it all depends on the roots and herbs you're working with, and the prayers and petitions you pray over the work. There are different categories of this type of domination work, such as Do as I Say, controlling, and Bend Over work. I know there are a lot of folks who think that this type of work is wrong. I was taught to believe that as long as a work is justified, it's okay to do the work. This is where discernment comes in. There are times when this type of work is needed. You may work at a job where your boss just walks all over you and, no matter what you do, you cannot please them. This would be the time to do Bend Over work so that you can bend their will and make them softer, and maybe even sugar them so they will be nice to you.

I'm not saying that you should run around dominating and controlling everybody that doesn't do what you want, because we have to remember every action causes a reaction. If the work is not justified, then you're taking a chance of getting hit with your own work. This type of magic is not something that you do on a whim; this is within the darker shades of magic because you are changing a person's free will. Some folks are not willing to go that far and that's okay. That's up to you, but I feel like personally this is work that needs to be known, because not everybody feels that it's wrong. There is a time and a place for this type of work.

Here's the other thing: Just because you know something does not mean you have to do it. I know a lot of stuff; that doesn't mean that I'm gonna jump in with both feet and do it, because every action causes a reaction and I am not doing anything that my spirits warn me against doing.

This is why discernment is so important in this work. Before I do any type of magical work, I either work with my pendulum, throw the bones, or pull three cards to see if I should even be entertaining the idea. I have learned when the Holy Spirit says "no," no means no. In those times when I did not listen because my feelings were involved in the situation, my behind got spanked. Most of the time it didn't happen instantly but, further down the road, my spirits reminded me of when I was told "no" and I did not listen.

This is for all the young workers out there: Be mindful of everything that you do. Use your common sense. You should never work when you're mad, especially when doing this type of work. Our words hold power, and they bring about change, and if it's not justified then you're no different than the person that you feel wronged you. Never jump in with both feet; work with spirit through divination, then listen to spirit and follow through. I know it's hard to be told no when you have so many feelings invested in whatever is going on, but sometimes you have to take a step back and put it in spirit's hands, and let them take care of the issue. They will handle the situation. Even if you don't see things moving the way you want them to, the Holy Spirit always brings justice when they are petitioned for justice to be served. You have to remember our time ain't God's time!

Enemy

Enemy work falls into the same category as domination work: controlling. Some folks consider it a darker type of magic. The thing is that any type of work, even cleansing work, can be considered a darker type of magic for the simple fact that when we cleanse ourselves we're removing whatever energy has been placed on us or that we have picked up. That energy we're removing is always gonna go back where it came from, and I truly believe this. One of the reasons that I believe this is because I have sat back and I have watched that when I do cleansing works and reversals, some folks whose worlds seem to be running fabulously all of a sudden start having issues, and I always think to myself, *huh, spirit always knows where to go*. So I don't look at any type of work as being light or dark; it's work.

Another thing is that once you give your problem over to the spirits that walk with you, it's out of your hands because those spirits are gonna take over and they're gonna do what needs to be done. So it's not actually *you* doing anything; you are simply asking the Holy Spirit to take care of a situation where you are being harmed. It's not our place to tell spirits how to do their job, and it's not our place to dictate to them after we have petitioned them to come to our aid and help us with a situation that we're having an issue with.

Being a Conjure woman, I don't look at things as being light or dark, or good or evil. I'll look at things being done with justification. If the work is justified, then it is the right work to be done, so therefore I don't look at enemy work as being dark or evil. I look at it as being able to claim justice against someone who threw unjustified work at me. We all have to answer for the things that we do, and we always have to remember that every action causes a reaction. When you harm someone for no reason, or just because you got in your feelings about something that they did or said, it still doesn't give you the right to do work on them just because you're feeling some kind of way. When you do unjustified work on someone, then that turns the work into dark magic because you are crossing someone up or jinxing someone who has done nothing wrong to you. Therefore, when they do cleansing or reversal or cutting-clear types of work, you are going to get hit with your work. That does not mean that they're throwing at you; that means that they are simply removing what was placed on their spirit that was unjustified.

So, in all things, think before you act. Know that there are works out there that can bring you justice. Sometimes it is better just to leave things alone and keep it moving!

Nail 'Em Down

Once again, here we are where the work is something that some folks consider dark magic. I have to disagree with that. There are times when folks need to sit the hell down. They're doing too much, they're causing too much confusion, they're causing too much drama and too much trauma in other folks' lives. If I do divination on a situation and spirit says that it is justified to do the work, I'm not going to think twice about nailing the target down.

I have been asked many times what I mean by "nail them down." I mean exactly that; you take a nail, you take their photo, and depending on why you are doing the work you nail them either facing the wall or face down on the floor, which totally blocks them from moving. They are literally up against the wall. You can also nail them down face up, which is a lighter, more sugary way of doing the work. But I'll be honest: If someone has pushed me to this point, I'm gonna put them flat, face down against the wall or on the floor, and just walk on their photo every time I pass by there.

There are also other ways that you can nail someone down without physically nailing them to the wall, to the floor, or maybe to a tree. You can place them under a rock. If you looked under my computer desk right now, you would see a big old rock there, and if you lifted that rock you might see a few photos under there that are facing down. (There might be one or two of them that are face up.)

This may seem too simple to work, but it works and it works well. You have to remember that the nail or the rock is not the one doing the work; spirit is. You could tie the photos up with a string and petition the spirit to stop them and to nail them down, and if you're in with your spirits like you're supposed to be, then even a string can stop them. Spirit will do whatever you ask them to do when it's justified and when it is meant for you.

I had an elder tell me one time that anything that you have to battle for and keep fighting for is not for you. Your blessings should not be a battlefield. Does that mean that spirit is just gonna hand you everything easy? No. Some things are just not meant for us to have. We may not see it, but spirit sees everything. That's why it's so important that you work with some type of divination tool before you do any type of work to see if you should be doing the work or not.

Some folks see an enemy at every turn and some folks don't see them at all because they don't do divination. They don't discern what is going on in their life in order to see why all these things are happening. Is it just a bit of bad luck, which we all have sometimes, or is it more? Is magic afoot causing the issues? You have to stay on top of your life. You should do a layout at least once a month. It can just be three cards pulled, but this will give you an idea of what is going on.

Heat Up Work

Sometimes it seems like our magic is stuck and that it's not moving. It could be because we didn't follow through with everything that spirit told us to do, or it could be because we're not doing the right type of work that we should be doing against the situation. It could be that the work that we've done doesn't have enough power to it to get the job done or as much power as we need it to have. When this happens, you can heat it up by adding fire to the work.

You can also add spicy roots and herbs to the work that put out heat. The only thing with using a lot of spicy roots and herbs is that the spicy stuff has a tendency to make the target hotheaded. I know y'all are tired of hearing me say this, but when this happens, this is when you go back and you do divination to see if you need to redo the work, or if you can just add a side work to heat some of the work to get the work moving.

You would not add heat to a few different types of work because it could make the magic too hot and cause more problems than are needed. Here's an example: If you are doing a peaceful-home work, then you would not want to heat that work up. You are trying to calm things down, not make them hotter. If you are dealing with a court-case work, and it seems like it's not going the way you need it to go, you would not heat the judge up. That's gonna make him aggravated and it's gonna throw the whole court case off. When you're in this type of situation, it's always better to just do some extra work to empower the work or to work alongside the work that you already have going, because sometimes too much heat causes a big blow up and makes folks hotheaded, and it just causes more issues than it's worth. It's much easier just to add a work to go along with the magic that you're doing that doesn't seem to be moving as fast as you would like for it to move.

Then again, we have to remember that our time is not God's time, and God truly decides how long something takes. There have been times when I've done work for someone sitting right here in front of me. They were waiting for a phone call from their husband, and before I could get the medicine bottle put together, the man was calling on the phone. It happened that fast. Then there've been times when I had to work really hard to make the job a success. Usually in those times it's when I myself didn't follow with what I was supposed to be doing, either because I just ignored spirit or I thought the way I was doing it was going to be the better way. Because sometimes spirit will give you a recipe or a work to do that doesn't make sense to you and you second-guess yourself and that's when you run into trouble. Just do the work as it is given to you, listen closely to what your spirits are trying to tell you, and your work will go a lot smoother. I learned this the hard way through experience.

Putting It on Ice

You will find that sometimes things get too hot, and, in those times, you have to literally put the work on ice. There are a lot of different types of work where you work with putting a target on ice or in the freezer or just in a cup of ice to settle them down and cool their heads. This is done when someone is out-of-control mad and hotheaded. There have been a few times in my life when I have literally had to put my own photo in the freezer because I was so upset and so mad. The thing is that when you are mad or you are hotheaded, you cannot think. All it does is cause a bunch of confusion and a bunch of aggravation. Think about it—when you're mad, all you have is tunnel vision, and you only see whatever the issue is. You can't fix the issue if you have tunnel vision and all you can feel is the fire of your anger or the upset of your emotions. I know this seems like something that is so simple that it could not possibly work but it does.

A lot of the peaceful homework goes along with cooling things off. This type of magic is what I call soothing magic; it brings peace and quietness. This is really some of my favorite work that I like to do. There's nothing like watching turmoil and aggravation turn into peace; it's a true blessing. One of the ways that you can cool things off in your home or your office is to get a ziplock bag with some lavender and a little bit of sugar. Add those ingredients to the ziplock bag. Then you can take a photo of either your home or inside your office or of the person who is causing the issue and place the photo into the ziplock bag. Fill it full of water, let out all the air where the bag is flat, and place it in the freezer. What you will find is, as the water freezes, the issue seems to just go away. This will give you a chance to do a stronger magic on the situation, but, for right now, it will bring the peace that you need to be able to think. This is a simple container magic that works.

Sweetening

Sweetening work is done to sweeten a person or a situation that is causing problems. It can be worked to bring peace to the home, and can even sweeten your money. This type of work is usually worked in a situation where things are not going the way you want them to go, especially if you are trying to get someone to do something for you or to take that extra step, go that extra mile to help you. If you are trying to buy a car, buy a house, get a loan—these are some of the situations where sweetening work, sweetening magic, could come in handy and help. Basically what you are doing is sweetening a person or a situation in your favor. This work can be done for court cases to pull the judge over to your side, to sweeten them, so they have sympathy for your case and the things that are going on. You can work on the loan officer at the bank that you're trying to get a loan from by sweetening them and throwing in a little bit of domination so that they see things the way you want them to see them.

Sweetening work can also sweeten your home life and bring peace, where you can have joy and happiness inside your own home. Simply place a photo of your home or your family in a bowl of sugar, sprinkle lavender over it, and place it on top of the icebox, the highest place in the kitchen, because the kitchen is the heart of the home. Lavender brings peace. It is soothing, so it is good for all types of work. I work with it a lot, even in the domination types of work, because it soothes the target. It keeps them from realizing what is really going on. If you came into my home, you would see lavender hanging on the wall in my kitchen over my kitchen sink where I do the dishes. It is also in my living room where we sit as a family because it does bring a soothing peace, and as far as I'm concerned, it should be added to all types of sweetening work, peaceful-home work, and when you are trying to achieve a goal to get something from someone. It soothes them and they let their guard down.

Souring

Souring work does exactly what it says: It will sour a person, place, or thing. This type of work is done when you are trying to cause friction between two people or cause an issue between two people, or you may want to sour someone's money. I don't recommend that. Folks have to eat, and it is not up to us to decide who has money issues and who doesn't! Most of the time, these folks are their own worst enemy and will do a great job of destroying themselves without any help. This type of work is done when you are trying to get rid of someone, to run them off, to separate a couple, or to sour someone's life who has done you wrong once. Again, this is what some folks call "dark magic," and I'm gonna have to repeat what I said: It's only dark if it's not justified. And you may be wondering, what in the world couldn't make this type of work justified? Well, I'll give you a couple of examples. What if someone were starting trouble for you on your job and they were good friends with the supervisor. The supervisor let them get away with everything, and you were on the verge of being fired because of this person. Do you think that souring the relationship between the person and your supervisor is not justified? Would you rather let this person continue to cause the issue between you and the person that could fire you for no apparent reason, or would you rather do the work and stop the situation?

Here's another example of when this work would be justified. If someone is sticking their nose in your relationship or your home life, and they are causing issues between you and your spouse, do you not feel like it is justified to separate them from your home? A lot of times our spouses don't see the damage that folks are doing to their relationship until it's too late. So in that instance, souring this person in the eyes of your spouse is more than justified. Or would you rather just let them continue interfering in your home life until your relationship is destroyed? Not all souring works are negative. In these two instances, souring work is a positive thing because it is moving the issue out of the way. It is all about justification.

One last example would be if you had a teacher at school who was bullying your child, and the principal always took the teacher's side and turned a blind eye toward whatever was going on between your child and that teacher. Would you not want to separate that situation? Wouldn't you want justice for your child? Do you care at this point if that teacher gets fired? So in order to handle that situation, you would need to sour the relationship between the teacher and the principal, and you would need to sweeten that principal toward you where they would listen to what you are trying to say and help your child. So not all work when you are dominating, controlling, or souring a situation is dark work. Some of these works are needed to bring forth justice to the party that is being wronged. Like I said before, just because you know how to do something doesn't mean you have to do it. If this type of work does not sit well with your sensibilities, then by all means don't do it, but you never know when you may need the knowledge of how to do this type of work. There may come a time when you are going to need to know how to do this type of work. Like the old folks say, just keep it in your back pocket, because you never know when you might need it!

Double Action

What exactly is a double-action work? I was taught that double-action works are works where you do more than one thing to achieve your goal. So if you're doing work to draw in money and prosperity, you could also do work to attract things that will draw in money and prosperity. If you have ever seen a candle that has two separate colors to it, that is a double-action candle. One color does one thing, and when it burns down to the next color, you change your petition to a petition that works with the other color in the wax. For instance, if you're doing a money blockbuster, and you're working with candles, the candle should be black on top and green on the bottom. That is a double-action candle. The goal of doing magic with that type of candle is twofold. It is to remove the blocks that could possibly be in your money, and then it is to draw money into your life when the blocks are clear.

As we know, black absorbs, so the top half of that candle is meant to absorb the cross conditions that had been placed on your money, or the jinx or the bad luck you're experiencing, so when you're praying your petition over that type of candle, you need two petitions. One petition is for spirit to remove all blocks, all cross conditions, all jinxes, anything that is in the way of your prosperity. You continue praying that petition until all the black wax in the candle is gone. Once you see the green wax, then it is time to change your petition up and to petition spirit to draw in the prosperity that you need. This is what a double-action work does. If you are burning this type of candle for prosperity, then you should also be doing work for protection. This puts this work as a double-action work. You're not only removing the issues that are there and drawing in the money, but you're also protecting that work and protecting that money.

I don't think that a lot of folks understand the difference between a double-action work, a triple-action work, and a reversal work. Reversal candles also have two different colors. They're made green and black for money, black and red for love or attraction, and you can find them sometimes in black and blue for healing work, and also in black and white for uncrossing work. They all basically work the same. The black wax absorbs the negativity, the cross conditions, or whatever the issue is that is going on, and the colored wax promotes whatever it is that you are trying to achieve. So if you are doing a healing candle and you work with the black and blue candle, then when you light the candle you start praying your petition that the illness be removed from you and that you are no longer ill. When it reaches the blue then your petition changes up, and you are petitioning God and the spirits that walk with you to give you good health. The black and blue candle can also be worked with for peaceful-home work. The black part represents the issues that are going on in the home and removing them out of the way, and the blue part represents the peace that you are praying for.

Triple Action

A triple-action work is any work that is done in threes. So if you are doing a reversal, a peaceful-home work, and a Do as I Say work all altogether, then that would be a triple-action work. I picked these situations because I think that it is a good example to explain. If you're having issues in your home and you do divination that shows someone is working against you and your home life, then you would do a reversal to send back whatever has been sent to you. That's the first work. Then, in order to get your house back to the state it used to be in where there was peace and you were able to relax and enjoy your home, you would do a peaceful-home work. Now, if I have to do a peaceful-home work in my home, I'm gonna get in control of the situation, therefore, I would do a Do as I Say or a controlling work to go along with the other two works I am already doing.

And I can hear someone reading this and saying, "Why would you need to do dark magic in order to bring peace to your home?" Anyone who has ever had an upset in their home knows that if you don't get control of the situation, it's just gonna fester and grow. I'm a heavy-handed worker and I don't like to do extra work, so if there have been a lot of fighting and arguing going on in my home, I am going to get total control over it because I want peace in my home. When you are dealing with a cross condition or a jinx or some type of black magic, then you have to get control of the situation. The only way to do that is to do a reversal and then a peaceful-home. Then do a spiritual cleansing on your home and everybody in it if you are gonna get control and just settle everybody down and let the reversal work do its job. It really is up to each individual how they do their work. My way is not the only way. I have found that it has worked for me doing work these types of ways so I'm gonna continue doing it. Like I said, the path of least resistance is always the best path.

Hotfoot

I spoke about hotfoot a little earlier, but I want to really go into detail here because I don't think that folks really understand what this work does when you hotfoot a target. Hotfoot should be the last resort, not the first one!

I think I have established that I am no sugary worker and that I will do whatever has to be done to get the job done, as long as it is justified. There are many different categories of hotfoot that folks should choose from, instead of instantly jumping into the harshest one in order to move someone out. There is a lot of information out there about how to do a hotfoot—about moving somebody out, moving them away from you—but there's not a lot of information that talks about what happens to the target. And I'm sure that you're thinking, "What does it matter?" It matters to me because not every person that has been hotfooted has been justified.

The reason I say this is because not every action deserves the reaction that hotfoot work causes. Yes, I sell hotfoot powder, and yes, I've been told it works wonderfully, and I'm sure it does. There are instances where hotfoot definitely should be worked, I'm not saying there aren't, but in some instances there are other ways to get a person moving down the road instead of fully hotfooting them.

When you work on someone with hotfoot powder or oil, it's going to move the target out if the product is made right, but it's also gonna keep that target unsettled. It could be years and years before they are able to settle down again. Are there some instances where this is justified? Yes, there are, but should everyone that we want to get away from us, or move out, or move down the road have to go through this? No, I don't feel like they do, especially when there are lighter ways to hotfoot someone and move them out of the way that don't cause the issues that hotfoot causes.

We are all responsible for everything that we do. If you use this type of work against a target and it is unjustified, trust and believe sooner or later it's gonna make its way back to you. Like the old folks say, "We reap what we sow," and hotfooting someone should be a last resort.

There are many works that can be done to move someone out of the way other than hotfooting them. **Hotfoot is a drastic measure.** Does your reasoning for this type of harsh work justify a drastic-measure kind of reaction? You need to ask yourself that before you get heavy-handed with hotfooting a target, because you are responsible for your own actions and you have to answer for them.

Here are a couple of different works that will achieve the same effect as using full-strength hotfoot, but that do not have the same residual effect as hotfoot work. If you have a situation and you need someone to move out of the way or you need to move them out of a house or a job, you can simply get a medicine bottle and some dirt from three spots that are pointing away from the house or the job. Get either the name of the target written on paper or a photo of the target burnt to ash. You add that photo or name paper and the dirt from the three corners and put some red pepper in that bottle.

Close the bottle up and put it in a candle setup with five red stick candles that have been dressed with castor oil and lightly powdered with red pepper. Don't get heavy-handed with that red pepper—if you do, it is going to run you out of there, because it's going to get hot and put off fumes that are gonna make you cough and make your eyes burn and water. It takes just a little bit.

Now set the medicine bottle down on the table and set the stick candles up exactly like this: Set the first candle at the top, the next one at the bottom, the third one to the right, and then the fourth one to the left. You go from right to left because you want this target to move out; you want them to move away from you. The last candle you're gonna set on top of the medicine bottle in a fireproof holder so that it doesn't melt the medicine bottle when the candle burns to the bottom, but it will still heat up the top of that medicine bottle.

You light each candle in the order that you set them down, so it will be top, bottom, right, left, then the candle that's sitting on top of the medicine bottle. As you light each candle, you say your prayer and your petition that the target leave and move on in peace—but in a hurry. You do this on each candle. The last candle is the candle that you are really working to get the target out of the way. When you light that candle, you call the target's name three times and you petition that they be moved out and moved away quickly.

Once the candles burn out, pick up the medicine bottle and shake it really hard. Call out the target's name and tell them that as long as they are where they should not be, they cannot rest. They have to leave, they want to go, and they want to go fast, fast, fast! You repeat this process for nine days. On the tenth day, you take the medicine bottle and either place it on a railroad track where the trains go (make sure that it is a working track that has trains moving back and forth on it) or throw the medicine bottle into a body of running water. If you do this work right and you are consistent, the target will move and leave, and there will be no need to hotfoot them. Just be wise in the type of work you do. Always use your common sense and just remember that you are responsible for every work you do.

GET YOUR MIND RIGHT

When I decide that I am going to do any type of work, the first thing I do is either work with my pendulum, work with the bones, or pull three cards to see if I should even be doing magic on the situation at all. When you are taking on the responsibility of changing folks' lives, you really should make sure that that is what you are supposed to be doing. Sometimes it's not our place to try to change things, or to make things go the way we want them to go. Sometimes it causes more harm than it does good. This is why discernment is so important in any type of magical working, no matter what it is, because sometimes you can make a situation worse if you're not supposed to do work on it. Sometimes the spirit already has the solution to the problem worked out and all you need to do is just sit back, relax, and let the spirit do its job.

I remember one time I was furious at someone who had truly done me wrong. There was no guessing about it, there was no wondering about it, there was no thinking about it; it was a fact and I wanted to act on it. I wanted revenge, I wanted justice, and I felt like I was owed justice. What made it worse for me is that when I did divination on the situation, spirit told me to sit my behind down and not to lift one finger toward the target. I tell you that was one of the hardest things that I have ever done: to put my faith in spirit and know they were going to handle the issue. Sometimes you have to listen, and when the answer is "no," do not do anything, no matter how hard it is. You have to do what your divination tells you to do.

You have to get your mind right in order for the job to be a success; you have to use discernment to make sure that you are on the right track. You can do all the spiritual work in the world, but if you do divination and you're told not to do it, there will be repercussions. That's a fact. Some folks call it karma. I call it reaping whatever you sow. But no matter what name you call it, if you do unjustified work, it will come back and bite you in the behind.

Life is not always fair, and magic is a serious thing that should never be played with. Just use caution and discernment when you are trying to find out if you should even perform the magic, or if you should let it go and let spirit handle it. If I get the okay to do a job, then it's time for me to get myself together and get myself prepared to do the work. The very first thing that I do is a spiritual cleansing on myself. You don't want to draw anything that is hanging around on you into the work that you are fixing to do. That's the very first step. Then I will gather up all the supplies that I need to do the job. I usually work with my pendulum to find out if the ingredients that I have picked are the right ingredients, and also to check and see if I need to add anything else to the work. It's important that you have a clear mind and you can think clearly when you are preparing to do a job. Once I gather everything I need, I will say my prayers over the ingredients I will be working with. I then set a candle burning in the middle of the ingredients.

The next day, I will do a brush down with either a chicken foot or one of my brooms I work with for cleansing work. When you work with a broom or a chicken foot to brush down to clear blocks and such out of the way, you start at the crown of the head and brush straight downward. Do not go back and forth because all you would be doing is mixing and moxing what you are trying to remove. The ingredients need to be prayed over and have a candle burnt on them for three days in order to get them ready to be worked. I was not taught to just throw everything together and then do the prayers in a setup. I think some folks don't even put their ingredients in a setup; from what I've been told they simply place them in whatever they're working on and then do their prayers. This is not how I was taught, even though I know that it is a faster way to work. From experience, I have learned when you pray over your ingredients before you put the work together it makes for a stronger work. Not only that; the work seems to hit faster and last longer.

Before I start doing any type of work, I always do a cleansing first. Then I will do a brush down every day when I am working on the work to make sure that nothing I've got going on ends up inside of the work. I know this sounds like a lot to do, but the benefit from it is success. You have to remember that nothing is free in this life. Everything costs something, whether it's money, time, knowledge—it costs something, so you might as well do the work right the first time. I don't like redoing work so I will go that extra mile in order to try to make sure that it's done right the first time.

When you are doing magic or Conjure, whatever you wanna call it, you should be focused on what you are doing, because if you get sidetracked it takes away from the energies that you are trying to pull into the work. You have to make sure that you are able to focus and really be into what you are doing. It really does make a difference. It seems like every time I personally try to work on something or get something going that I need to get done, everybody and their brother wants to call and text or just interrupt what I'm doing, so you have to stay focused.

Another thing that I wanna touch on in this section, since we are talking about getting yourself together in order to do your work, is to try to make sure that you don't have a lot of stress and aggravation going on when you're trying to work, because you will draw that into your work. We all have those days and we all have work that we have to get done, but you have to make sure that your mind is in the right space when you're doing any type of magic because you are praying. You are focused on what you're doing. Prayers draw spirits, and you have to be careful because you don't know what you're gonna pull in there when your feelings are not where they're supposed to be. So make sure that your mind is right and your spirit is cleansed before you take on spiritual work.

I also want to share how I start my work and the steps that I take. Some may already work like this, some may not. You may have your way of doing things, but not everybody who reads this book is going to know how to get their self together before they start working.

Like I've said before, the very first step is to do a divination to see if I should even be doing the work. For me, this is the most important part. I have learned from past mistakes that when spirit says "no," they really mean no. If the divination shows it's favorable to do the work, then I will sit with a burning candle and a glass of water and petition spirit to show me the right way to do this job at this time. I work with my pendulum to make sure that I'm on track, and I ask questions to make sure that I am really hearing what they are saying. I have a pen and paper and I write down the ingredients that I am hearing, and then I will ask again if these are the ingredients that I should be adding to this work.

Once I have written down everything that I need for the job, then I have to decide how I am going to do the work. Is this gonna be something that's ongoing? Is it gonna be something that's gonna have to continually be worked? Once again, divination is my friend. I will usually use my cards for this. While I shuffle, I ask my questions, then I pull three cards. Whatever those three cards tell me is how I'm going to go. If it is a long-term work, I will put it either in a handkerchief or some other type of container.

Container work is the best work to work with when you are working a long-term job, because the more you work the container, the stronger the work becomes, and the longer the magic lasts. If you leave your work just sitting, eventually all the magic is gonna be drained out of it, but if you keep working and feeding it, that magic is going to get stronger and stronger. For me, a job is not done until I have successful results.

Once I know exactly what I am doing and how I am going to do it, then I think about the situation and the prayers that need to be said over the work. Not every prayer fits every work. Sometimes you have to change the petition up to match the prayer, so that's my next step. Once I figure that out, then I think about when the right time is to do the work. Usually if I'm drawing something in, I will do the work when the sun is coming up, and if that's too early or something else is going on, I will have it done by the time the sun is high in the sky, which is high noon. If I am removing something or nailing something down, then I will start that work in the afternoon when the sun starts going down. So sunrise till noon when you're drawing in, afternoon 'til five o'clock when the sun is going down when you're removing or nailing something down because you're trying to stop it.

I don't necessarily work with the moon phases because that's not how I was taught. I work with the hands of the clock. When the hands of the clock are moving upward from six o'clock 'til noon, I'm good when I'm doing drawing work. When the hands of the clock are moving from around 12:05 p.m. on down, then I'm good to do removing or nailing down work. By the time the hands reach down 12:30 p.m., then they start going back up—in that thirty minutes you need to have your work started.

When I am working on a petition for a work, I don't use a lot of words. You don't have to fill that petition full of a bunch of words, because too many words tend to confuse spirit and they really just get in the way. I have found the best way is to use power words. They are words that hold power in them, like money, love, protection and so on. You don't need to fill a page when you write your petition. The best way is to get straight to the point and build those into the petition. The petition is a big part of the work because that is the foundation that you are trying to build off of. Your Bible verses are another strong part of the work because they help tell spirit what you are trying to achieve. The verse below, Jeremiah 32 V 17, is one of my favorite verses for drawing in power when I'm getting ready to start a work. The end of the verse says nothing is too hard for you, which means you can do anything that you want to because God gives you the power to do it.

Jeremiah 32 V 17

> Ah, Sovereign Lord, you have made the heavens and the earth by your great power and outstretched arm. Nothing is too hard for you.

Pick a prayer that fits what is going on—not every prayer fits every situation. You have to get into the Bible and find your prayer. The best way to do that is Bibliomancy, which is the art of getting answers out of the Bible. It is not hard to work with the Bible in this way. When I need to find answers that I can't find anywhere else or understand something that I cannot seem to figure out, I will go to the Bible. The way I was taught Bibliomancy was to hold the Bible between both hands, blow three breaths over the it, say your petition three times, and then open the Bible. Look down wherever your eyes fall and start reading that verse. Nine times out of ten, you're gonna find the answer that you're looking for. This is just another way of being able to discern what spirit is trying to tell you. It's simple, easy, and no hocus-pocus.

Once you have everything together, then it's time for you to start gathering up all your ingredients and start toward doing the work. It depends on the work and what I am trying to achieve as to how many days I do the work. It could be three, five, seven, nine, or twenty-one days. It just all depends on what the divination tells me, on my interpretation of what spirit is telling me, and on my knowledge from other works that I have done in the past that are similar to whatever I am working on.

My normal prayers that I work with every day are the Our Father or Lord's Prayer, Hail Mary, the Apostles' Creed, and Psalm 23. I say each one three times. I light a white stick candle and have a cool glass of water sitting on the table for spirit while I am praying. These are my daily morning, noon, and night prayers. Doing this daily helps me get into the right frame of mind to start my day. It also gives back to spirit for the blessings they bestow on me daily and shows how grateful I am.

PRAYERS

You shouldn't have to get ready to do magic; you should stay ready. The way you do this is to stay prayed up, to stay honoring the spirits that walk with you. Make it become a daily habit. You will be surprised how empowered you will become because every day you are feeding spirit and they are feeding you, so it makes it easier to reach your goals, easier for your life to run smoothly, and when things happen they don't seem as bad because you are prayed up. You do have that holy power walking with you. I know there're a lot of folks that are not Christians, but it doesn't matter. A holy power is a holy power; it doesn't matter what name you call it; the energy and the strength and the power are all the same.

I'm gonna place the prayers I pray daily below just for convenience, 'cause I know some folks don't know these prayers. You don't have to use them, you can pray whatever you wanna pray, but they're gonna be here if you need them.

The Our Father

Our Father, Who art in heaven, hallowed be Thy name; Thy kingdom come; Thy will be done on earth as it is in heaven. Give us this day our daily bread; and forgive us our trespasses as we forgive those who trespass against us; and lead us not into temptation, but deliver us from evil. Amen.

Hail Mary

Hail Mary, full of grace. The Lord is with thee. Blessed art thou amongst women, and blessed is the fruit of thy womb, Jesus. Holy Mary, Mother of God, pray for us sinners, now and at the hour of our death. Amen.

The Apostles' Creed

I believe in God,
the Father almighty,
Creator of heaven and earth,
and in Jesus Christ, his only Son, our Lord,
who was conceived by the Holy Spirit,
born of the Virgin Mary,
suffered under Pontius Pilate,
was crucified, died, and was buried;
he descended into hell;
on the third day he rose again from the dead;

he ascended into heaven
and is seated at the right hand of God the Father almighty;
from there he will come to judge the living and the dead.
I believe in the Holy Spirit,
the holy catholic Church,
the communion of saints,
the forgiveness of sins,
the resurrection of the body,
and life everlasting. Amen.

Psalm 23

The LORD is my shepherd; I shall not be in want. He restores my soul. He guides me in paths of righteousness for his name's sake. Even though I walk through the valley of the shadow of death, I will fear no evil, for you are with me; your rod and your staff, they comfort me. You prepare a table before me in the presence of my enemies; you anoint my head with oil; my cup overflows. Surely goodness and mercy shall follow me all the days of my life, and I shall dwell in the house of the Lord forever. Amen.

COMMON HERBS AND ROOTS I WORK WITH

This is by no means a full list of herbs and roots, but it is a list that I work with often, and most you'll find mentioned in this book as part of a particular Work. For a full list of roots and herbs that you can work with, you need to buy yourself a good herbal (I suggest my book *Hoodoo Herbal*). I just want to touch on these to give you a good foundation to start with.

Allheal can be added to baths for healing. It is also good when added to packets to keep sickness away.

Aloe is a very bitter herb that is added to Shut Your Mouth products and also added to works to stop gossip.

Alum is another one that can be worked with to stop gossip, but it is also good for removing cross conditions.

Angelica root, or what some call the Holy Ghost root, is the root of the angels. It is worked with for protection, when dealing with children who will not listen, and other family issues.

Asafetida stinks to high heaven. The old folks say that even the devil can't stand the smell of it, so this herb is worked with for Run Devil Run work and removing any cross condition.

Balm of Gilead, like lavender, is one of my favorite herbs to work with when I'm doing peaceful-home work or works to bring peace. It soothes hurt feelings and is also good when you are doing cut-and-clear work.

Barberry does exactly what the name implies: It bars things, stops them. This is a must-have in your cabinet. You can mix barberry, dirt from the four corners of a crossroads, and dirt from a stop sign to stop your enemies in their tracks.

Basil can be worked with for cleansings, to send evil away, for protection, and for healing. It is one of my favorite herbs to work with.

Bayberry is good for better business works, for drawing money into your pocket. There's a little rhyme that says, "Bayberry candle burned to the socket will put money into your pocket." It is a powerful money herb.

Bay leaf is good for protection and cleansing. A bay leaf placed behind the door will protect the home. One placed in every corner of the home will also offer protection. They are also good to add to cleansing baths and washes.

Bitter weed grows wild. It is worked with to sour a situation or a person, or make a person or situation bitter and unforgiving.

Blackberry leaves are worked with for all reversal work. They return the evil back to the sender. It is an important herb to have in your cabinet.

Bloodroot is worked with for all types of works dealing with your children or your family. It is good to add to peaceful-home works.

Broom straw is good for all types of cleansing work and protection work, and it's worked with to remove cross conditions.

Calamus root is worked with for all domination work or controlling works, such as Do as I Say works.

Cayenne pepper is added to heat things up. It puts fire in any work. Cayenne pepper should never be added to peaceful-home types of work because it's just going to heat up the temperament that's already going on in the home.

Couch grass can be worked with along with barberry to bind your enemies.

Damiana is an herb that is worked with in love and caring works. It can also be worked with when doing attraction and drawing works.

Deer's-tongue is worked with in court cases when you want to charm someone in love work. It helps you speak with eloquence.

Devil's bit is used as medicine and to heal.

Devil's claw is good for a new job, good luck, binding, and protection.

Devil's shoestring is powerful magic. The long stringy roots can "trip up" your enemies or the devil. It's often carried for protection against harm and negative energies.

Dirt dauber's nest is a small dirt nest that comes from the dirt dauber or mud dauber wasp. It is worked with for protection, domination, and controlling works.

Dragon's blood root is a good wound healer.

Eyebright is worked with as a wash to heal your eyes, but it also works well with Saint Lucy when you are trying to see what is going on. It works on anything that has to do with the eyes or seeing.

Five finger grass does anything that the five fingers on a hand can do, which makes it perfect for all types of money works and works where you are trying to draw something into your hands.

Gumbo filé is good for all money work, prosperity work, and success work.

High John root is used to draw money and luck, boost confidence, gain mastery and success, and to strengthen the male nature.

Jezebel root is worked with to make a man give you his money and for domination. It is another one of my favorite roots.

Job's tears are very powerful. They say that if you work seven seeds for seven days, they will make your wishes come true. On the other side of that, they can make your enemies shed tears.

Knotweed is worked with for all blocking and binding works.

Lavender is worked with to soothe feelings, bring peace, and to remove hurt feelings in a relationship.

Licorice root is worked with in all workings where you need power, strength to be in control, and to have domination over the situation. It is one of my all-time favorite roots.

Life Everlasting is good to add to all healing works. The old folks say that this herb will help you live a longer life.

Lovage root not only draws in love but also promotes self-love and should be added to all love works and healing works. A must for your cabinet.

Lucky hand root is added to all money works and is good for gambling. It is said to be a very lucky root.

Master of the Woods is good for all domination, controlling, and Do as I Say work.

Master root helps you take charge. It is great for all works that you need the upper hand in.

Motherwort is good for all types of work that is concerning your children or grandchildren.

Black mustard seeds cause confusion and loss of concentration when the work is being done on a target.

Nutmeg is worked with for all money matters and all things dealing with prosperity and good fortune.

Orange peel is worked with for all attraction works. It is one of the main ingredients in attraction products and road-opening products.

Queen Elizabeth root is worked with by women to draw power, love, luck, and the opposite sex. It also adds to a woman's personal power.

Ruda is worked with to remove all cross conditions. It can add power to the work. It can be worked with to destroy an enemy. It is good to grow ruda around your home to protect your home.

Self-heal is worked with in all health matters and is said to help cleanse.

Slippery elm is an herb that is worked with when you have folks gossiping about you or spiritually attacking you. This herb hides you from the enemy.

Snakeroot is worked with to stop gossip. It will also protect you against false friends. Everyone should have some of this planted at their homes. It's easy to grow.

Solomon's seal root is named after King Solomon in the Bible. It brings forth wisdom and power and adds protection in all Conjure work.

Spanish moss can be worked with to protect your money, your home—but it can also be worked with to nail an enemy down.

Tobacco can be used as an offering or to hold an enemy down.

Walnut is worked with to remove jinxes and cross conditions. It can also be helpful with breakup work.

Willow is worked with to help remove cross conditions and also to place a jinx on a target.

About Oils

In the works that follow, the directions will often include dressing your container with oil; I usually just indicate using a spiritual oil. The most basic spiritual oil is olive oil. Olive oil is a most holy oil. It is found all through God's word in the Bible. Olive oil and castor oil are good all-purpose dressing oils. Sometimes you'll need to use a specific oil, like money-drawing oil, success oil, or a protection oil. You can make specific dressing oils by adding some of the above roots and herbs to any type of base oil. Here is a small list of oils that can be used as base oil:

Almond oil
Castor oil
Coconut oil
Grapeseed oil
Jojoba oil
Mineral oil
Sunflower seed oil
Sweet oil (olive oil)

Refer to my book *Hoodoo Herbal* for more indepth instructions and recipes for creating oils for specific purposes.

THE WORK

Apples

To Keep Love Alive

This work can be done to keep the love alive in a relationship. If you feel your lover is slipping away from you, then try this work. It not only sweetens the relationship, but as the ivy grows, so does their love for you grow. I like to do this work with ivy because the ivy is hardy and it clings. It can also be done with a miniature rose bush because it can be kept in a pot. The rose bush is also good because it has thorns, which will protect your love. I have a client who planted hers under a jasmine plant.

You can choose where you want to plant your apple. Like I said, I prefer the ivy. My ivy is planted in a large pot next to my front door. I keep my plant by the front door so the ivy grows alongside the door, which keeps him coming back through the door.

For this work you will need

- a glass bowl
- a large red apple
- a photo of the two of you when y'all were happy
- three red stick candles
- a pinch of lovage root
- a pinch of licorice root
- a pinch of lavender

Make sure the couple is facing each other in the photo. You will also need some kind of spiritual oil, a little bit of whiskey, and some powdered sugar. You need to take one of the Bible verses below out of the Bible and burn it to ash. Now, before you get all up in arms about burning a page out of the Bible, if you really know your Bible you know that the word of God cannot be burnt. Even though the paper is burned, you will still be able to see God's word. Mix the ash with the other ingredients, then you place the ingredients on top of the photo. Then you fold the photo toward you and make a small packet. You can either run a pin through the photo to hold it together, or you can use red cotton string to bind the photo together. This now becomes a packet. Try to make it as small as possible because the packet is gonna go inside of the cored apple.

Core the top of the apple. Make sure that you cut deep enough inside of the apple without splitting the apple, then you place the packet in the apple. Place the apple in the bowl. Using a nail, write on the first stick candle *the Lord is my shepherd; I shall not want*. It doesn't matter if you can read it or not. Dress the candle with some type of spiritual oil and lightly roll it in some powdered sugar. Hold the candle close to your mouth and pray over it. You will pray your personal prayer and one of the prayers that I have added for you to work with. Just to clarify because I have had folks ask me before what a personal prayer is: A personal prayer is a prayer that you pray in your own words from your heart.

Stick the candle end into that apple. If you are worried about the packet catching on fire, place a small piece of tinfoil over the packet just to be safe. And I can't stress enough that you need to watch as the candle burns because it could be a fire hazard. You should never leave a candle burning unattended. Sprinkle a little powdered sugar around the apple and pour a little bit of whiskey in the bowl. Say your prayer again then light your candle. You are going to pray over this work three times while the candle is burning.

You will repeat the work for three days, burning one candle each day. After the third candle burns out, leave the apple on the altar until the next day. You need to get a new pot, a plant, and some potting soil. Make sure that you get new things. The pot, the plant, and the potting soil all need to be new because you are trying to start fresh, so you don't want to use a plant or a pot or even the potting soil from an old plant that's been sitting around the house picking up all this energy that's been going on in your home between the two of you.

Rinse the new pot off with some cool running water to clear away any type of energy the pot might have picked up. Put a little bit of potting soil in the bottom of the pot, set the apple on top of the potting soil, then add some more potting soil until the apple is covered. Then you transfer your new plant into the pot on top of the apple. Finish covering the plant with potting soil. Make sure that you water the plant well after it is planted in the pot. The idea of this is that as the plant grows so shall your love grow stronger.

It's important that you keep this plant in good health and that you take care of it because the plant has basically become part of your relationship, and as you take care of the new plant you are taking care of your new relationship. Every time you water the plant, you say your prayer and your petition over the plant. Once a month, you can light a red stick candle that you have rolled in powdered sugar, just like you did in the beginning. This way you keep the fire going.

Bible Verses

Ephesians 5 V 33

However, each one of you also must love his wife as he loves himself, and the wife must respect her husband.

Song of Solomon 8 V 6

Place me like a seal over your heart,
like a seal on your arm;
for love is as strong as death,
its jealousy[a] unyielding as the grave.
It burns like blazing fire,
like a mighty flame.

Song of Solomon 4 V 10

How delightful is your love, my sister, my bride!
How much more pleasing is your love than wine,
and the fragrance of your perfume
more than any spice!

Song of Solomon 2 V 16

My beloved is mine and I am his;
he browses among the lilies.

Love Apple Plate

If you are trying to draw love into your life, the Love Apple Plate may be just the work you need. Who would have ever thought an apple could become a container? You need

- a nice juicy, large red apple
- a white plate
- five tea lights
- a photograph of the target
- your petition
- a magnet
- some sugar
- some red wine
- some lovage root

Before you start this work, you need to do at least one cleansing. This could be with an egg, a broom, a chicken foot, or you could do a cleansing bath. Once you have all your ingredients together, you need to say your regular prayers and then you can start to work.

Core the center out of the apple, then set the apple in the middle of the plate. Burn the photo of the target and the petition to ash, and mix the lovage root, sugar, and ash all together, then add the mixture into the apple. Place the plate with the apple in the center of a table, then you are going to place your tea lights around it. The placement is top to bottom, right to left. The reason that we are putting them right to left instead of left to right is because it is not time yet to nail this work down because you're sending the spirit out to pull the target to you, so the roads have to be open. You place the last tea light on top of the apple.

Tea lights are good for this type of magic for a couple of different reasons. One, the tin gets very hot so it heats the work up, and two, it is less of a fire hazard because the flame is contained within the small tin cup.

Once you have your candles laid down, it's time to pour the wine onto the plate around the apple. This will help feed the work. Then you light the tea lights in the order you set them down, so it will be top to bottom, right to left, and then the center one. Before you light each candle, you should say your prayer and your petition over the candle three times. Then you light that candle, you move on to the next one, and you repeat the prayers again three times until you have said the prayers over each of the candles.

Once all the candles are lit, you will need to say your prayers over the whole entire work again three times and preferably repeat the process three times during the day, which means another set of tea lights being placed on and around the work. It may seem like a lot of work but it takes work to have success, especially when you are doing love work. And I know some folks feel like it's wrong to do love magic on a target, but everyone has to follow their own convictions. What might not be right for one could save another person. Like I always say and my elder said to me: Just because you know how to do something doesn't mean you have to do it. You have to work with your own judgments when doing this type of work.

Apple-Head Work for Success

Some of the best work I have done has been for success. For me it's easy to work because I wanna see everyone I deal with be successful.

When folks are successful and their lives are going great, they don't seem to have a tendency to be jealous or envious of what others have. They are too busy trying to keep their own life together.

This work is made from a dried apple head. You need a large red apple and some lemon juice. You peel the apple and then you let it soak in the lemon juice for at least twenty-four hours. The next day you're going to take that apple out of the lemon juice and you are going to start to shape the face. All you have to do is pinch the nose and shape the mouth. Most of the time the eyes will already be noticeable. You can also use a knife to add more detail to the facial features. While you are shaping the face of the doll head, you should be praying for power, wisdom, and strength. Focus on where you want your life to move forward; don't focus on what you don't have.

Once you get the head shaped, you can place it in the oven at 125 degrees until it is completely dry. Or you can do it the old way and place it on a windowsill and just let the sun dry it naturally. This is how the apple-head dollies were made when I was growing up and every day you would shape the face a little bit until the head was completely dry. Once the head is completely dry, hollow out a hole in the bottom of the head. You will need to do one cleansing bath so your spirit can be cleansed and fresh, then take a photo of yourself and print it out. Below you will find an easy bath recipe so you can take a cleansing bath before you take your photo. I'm adding the recipe because not everyone who reads this may know how to put a cleansing bath together.

For this bath you need

a cup of strong black coffee
four tablespoons of baking soda
one cup of lemon juice

You add all the ingredients into the bath after you have taken your regular shower first. You should never take a cleansing bath with a dirty body. You need to pray the Isaiah 41 and Psalms 23. You can do this before, after, or during the bath. Once you get out of the bath, just pat yourself dry. Don't brush your body vigorously with the towel.

The next day, you are gonna gather all your ingredients so you can load the doll's head. You need to burn the photo of yourself to ash. Add in a pinch of hair from the crown of your head. You will need

- a pinch of Solomon's Seal root for wisdom
- lovage root for self-love
- mustard seeds to plant the seed of faith and total success in yourself
- a pinch of Master of the Woods to gain the upper hand
- a pinch of angelica root for healing
- a pinch of calamus root for power
- a pinch of five finger grass to open your hands so that you can grab prosperity, healing, and total success in your life

Just a small pinch of each ingredient will do. Then hold your ingredients in the palm of your hand and pray your petition over them. This petition is very personal, so say whatever you feel in your heart. The next step is to load the ingredients into the bottom of your apple-head doll. You will also need a small piece of cloth so you can close the bottom of the dollie head to hold the ingredients in once you get the head loaded.

Once you have the apple head loaded and sealed at the bottom, hold the apple head in your hands close to your mouth and state your full birth name and your petition over the head three times. Then place the apple head in the center of a clay plate. You can get the clay plates at the garden center; they should not be hard to find. Sprinkle some powdered sugar on the plate, starting at the edge of the plate and moving inward toward the center. You will do this in the sign of a cross, so you will start at the top of the plate going downward, then go to the bottom of the plate coming upward, because you are only going from the outside edges in, you're not putting the sugar on the doll head. Then you will start on the corner of the right side and come inward, then the corner of the left side and come inward.

When you have the powdered sugar down, it is time to lay down the tea lights that you have dressed with success oil. You set the tea lights down top to bottom, right to left, and one in the center of the plate, which should be sitting right on top of the dollie's head. Light the tea lights in the same order that you laid them out in, then you say your prayers and your petition over the dollie's head.

You are going to do the same setup for twenty-one days. After the twenty-one days, you need to wrap the doll head up and place it in a safe place. You also need to understand that this doll now represents you. It's gonna help with a couple of things, and it's also going to be a target if someone decides to throw at you, so it's also for protection.

This doll can also be worked to sweeten your head. Lovage root would be the main ingredient in this type of work because it promotes self-love. This type of dollie would benefit those who are suffering from low self-esteem and need to love themselves more. If you are interested in making one of these self-esteem heads for yourself, then I suggest you do a set of four cleansing baths, before you start. Once you've done your baths then take a fresh photo of yourself and start your work. You should also do a set of at least three cleansing baths once a month if you feel you are undeserving.

We should always think highly of ourselves and love ourselves. With this apple-head dollie you will have a good start toward getting your self-esteem back up where it should be. Once you have worked your dollie for a while, you can place the doll head in an ivy plant so as the plant grows, your self-esteem and your love for yourself will grow. Just make sure you keep the plant alive. If the plant dies, the magic dies. This is an easy way to help with the struggles of low self-esteem.

B

Beef Tongue

I wanted to share a work I did, but I also wanted to clear up a little misconception about this work. Some folks think when you do a beef tongue to shut someone up that all you have to do is fill the tongue and wrap it up. This is absolutely not true. I'll explain why. If you are going to shut someone's mouth and stop them from bothering you with their gossip, then you need to sew the tongue shut. As in sewing their mouth shut!

All old-school workers are taught this when they are taught shut-up work. I'm not sure where this wrapping thing came from, but if you, want to shut someone's lips and stop them from gossiping about you then you need to sew those lips closed. Common sense will tell you this. When this type of work is called for, all the ingredients are loaded into the tongue. You then sew up the slit in the tongue. This represents sewing up the target's mouth. Most of the time, if this work is done right, the target will feel a burning effect in their mouth every time they talk about you, and they may or may not know how to do reversal work. If the work is justified, they can do all the reversal work they want to do and it's not gonna change a thing. I've had folks tell me they have gotten blisters in their mouth because they think someone has tried to shut them up. I have also heard folks say that their mouth and their tongue will just start burning.

This work is easy to do and it works. The only problem is if it is unjustified and a reversal work is done for the target, then the worker will get a taste of their own medicine. That is why it is so important to do some type of divination—either cards, bones, or pendulum—to make sure that you are justified in doing any types of work like this. If you are unjustified then you do take a chance of getting hit with your own work, or spirit may decide to teach you a lesson. You and you alone are responsible for all the work you do, and remember, every action causes a reaction.

If you have a case where you need to do a Shut Your Mouth work on someone who is talking against you, this is an easy work to do. I was taught to soak the tongue in a wash of red peppers, cream of tartar, and alum. Not only is this recipe hot, it's also bitter. You should soak the tongue in the ingredients for at least twenty-four hours before you start to prepare the tongue for the work. I have seen some old workers blend the ingredients into a paste and cover the whole tongue with the paste after the tongue was loaded with the personal concerns of the target. If you decide to work with them with a paste instead of the wash, make sure to wear gloves, because those chili peppers get super hot and if you touch your face or your eyes with your hands, you are going to be on fire.

If you decide to soak the tongue in the ingredients for twenty-four hours, take the tongue out once the time is up, pat it dry, and then use a sharp knife to slit the tongue. The illustration on page 80 will show what it should look like.

Then you can either burn the target's photo to ash or you can place their photo in the slit. Then you add the other ingredients into the opening. It always depends on what spirit leads you to add, but

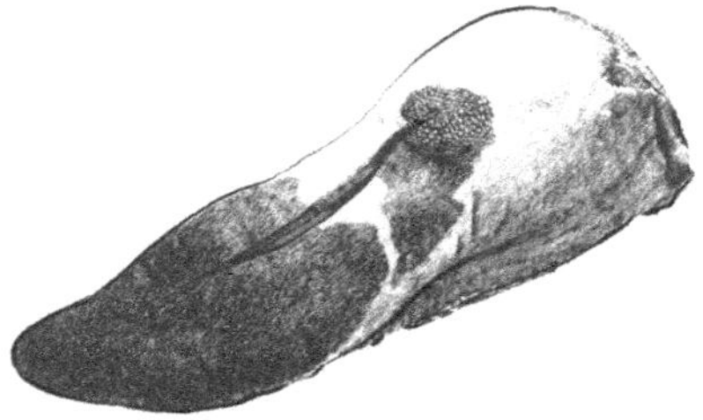

a shut your mouth work always has hot and bitter ingredients added to it. This work can be done for many different reasons, so the ingredients depend on the reason why you are doing it. Once the tongue is loaded, you will need a sharp needle to stitch it shut. On the first stitch you are going to make three knots: on the first knot you say, "In the name of God the Father"; on the second knot you say, "In the name of God, the Son";, and on the third knot you say, "In the name of God, the Holy Spirit." On each stitch after that you will pray your petition that your target keeps their mouth shut and stops talking about you and harassing you. If they choose not to, every time they speak your name, their mouth will burn and nothing will put the fire out. This is so they will not be able to continue to speak about you. If they do, they will start having issues with their teeth and their mouth.

When you have the tongue ready, then it is time to place it in a candle setup. For this work, you will make a circle of tea lights around the tongue. Inside the circle you will make a cross setup. Use five tea lights and place them in the shape of a cross: three tea lights in a vertical row, and then two candles are placed on each side of the vertical row. So when you look at it, it looks like you have three tea lights going downward and three tea lights going across. As you light the tea lights, say your prayer and petition over each tea light. You have to remember that any multiple of the number three is a powerful number.

Do the prayer work for three days. On the fourth day, it's time to nail the tongue to a tree or a post. You need three nails. You're going to nail the tongue to a tree or a post three days in a row. So the first day, you take the nail, the hammer, and the tongue, and you find a spot where you want to nail the tongue down. You say your prayers and your petition, and then take the nail and you put it at the tip of the tongue. Hit it with a hammer as you say, "I nail (so and so's name) tongue, just like Jesus's right hand was nailed to the cross." On the second day, you take your nail and your hammer and go a little ways down from the first nail. This can be a little tricky 'cause the tongue gets thicker. You say, "I nail the second nail in just like the nail that nailed Jesus left hand to the cross." On the third and last day you take your nail and your hammer and you move down from the second nail. As you nail the last nail in, you say, "I nail this tongue down just like Jesus's feet were nailed to the cross."

The work is now done. You just leave it there and let it do its job. It is still going to continue to work when it falls off the tree. Animals are gonna get it. They're gonna eat it and then they're gonna poop it out, so there goes your gossipmonger. Now I'm sure some folks will have some things to say about the prayer when you're nailing the nails into the tongue. This is Conjure work, folks. This ain't sugar and spice work, and the Bible is not full of all love and light. Like I always say, just because you know something doesn't mean you have to work with it, so if this work gets a hold of your sensibilities then just keep it moving. That's what I do, but understand this works. It is nothing to play with and you have to be sure that it is justified. If someone comes and tells you that someone is talking about you, then do a divination to see if this is actually the case or if it's just someone trying to cause a problem. You are the only one that is responsible for your actions. You can't blame it on nobody else, so be mindful of the works that you do.

The same way you can heat up a tongue that is talking about you to shut them up, you can also sweeten someone's tongue toward you. It's basically the same steps; only the ingredients that are placed in the tongue and that make the wash to soak the tongue are changed. I'm just gonna touch on it here, but I wrote about it in my book *Hoodoo Your Love*. This type of work is done when you are trying to sweeten someone's mouth toward you. It could be a coworker, it could be a boss, it could be a partner that is not speaking well toward you. I have found that the best ingredients for this type of work is a little calamus, two different types of sugar, and lavender if this has something to do with love. You could also add some white roses. You would make a wash of these ingredients and soak the tongue just like you would if you were doing a Shut Your Mouth work. Once the tongue has soaked for twenty-four hours, you would take it out, pat it dry, and load the ingredients into the tongue along with the target's photo. You could even make a paste and just cover the whole tongue with the paste if you chose not to soak the tongue for the twenty-four hours.

The difference in this work and Shut Your Mouth work is that this tongue needs to be placed in the freezer. If there ever comes a time when you no longer need the tongue to do the work for you, you simply defrost the tongue, remove all the ingredients, bury the ingredients in the east, and dispose of the tongue in a wild, wooded area.

Bird's Nest

If you have grown up within the Southern culture, then you know there are a lot of tales around bird's nests. One of the most memorable ones is to never cut or throw your hair outside because the birds could steal it for their nest. The old folks will tell you that if you allow your hair to be built into a nest, you could start to suffer with severe headaches and nightmares. They will also tell you that if you have severe nightmares, you should place an open Bible under your pillow or under your bed.

Bird's nests are worked with to lock something or someone down, or for protection. If you find a bird's nest, you can work that nest for protection of you and your home. You have to find an empty, abandoned one, though; you can't just steal a bird's nest. That would surely bring you bad luck. To work the nest, you take a photo of you and your home and you weave it into the bird's nest. Then you place that bird's nest over your front door.

The idea behind this is that in order for the work to get to you or to reach your home, it has to get through all the weaving of that bird's nest. Birds work hard to make those nests. They literally weave the pieces one by one to make a strong nest to hold their family, so in turn why wouldn't you work with that nest to protect your home and your family?

The bird's nest can also be worked to lock something or someone down. You can work with either the target's name or their photo. You burn the target's name or their photo into ash and then you mix that ash with lard. You rub that mixture inside the bird's nest so pieces of the target are trapped within that nest. They can't get out. The old folks say that when something is trapped, that spirit can only count so high and then they have to start over again, so there's no way that target is getting out of that trap.

Another way you can work that is to simply weave the target in between the sticks of the trap. That way you can work with that bird's nest over and over again. Just trap the targets in the nest so they can't get out. I'm sure you get the idea of it.

It is also a good idea to be very respectful of birds and their nests. Some folks say that some birds have a long memory. Just always be mindful of the work that you do and your own actions.

Loaded Big Mama Doll

I have always been drawn to dolls ever since I was a small child, even though growing up I don't remember ever having a doll other than the ones that were handmade by my grandma or one of my aunties. There was a time when I collected dolls, all kinds of beautiful dolls. They took over my life, I guess because there was never any money for dolls when I was growing up. I was grown, so I could afford to buy a new doll every once in a while. I ended up giving them all away to my granddaughters.

I'm a worker, so when I do a job sometimes a dollie is the only way to go. If you pray over the doll and you work the doll, the doll becomes part of the person you are either doing the work for or doing the work on. My grandma used to make what she called sock dollies. She would make us dolls out of old socks. I remembered watching her make these dolls, so I upped the game a little bit and, although my dolls are not exactly like hers, they're similar.

I called these dolls Big Mamas. Some folks call them La Madama dolls. They are working dolls. I have them on my website and I sell them to folks who need protection, prosperity, or who need different types of conditions drawn into their lives.

These dolls are loaded with petition prayers, photos, roots, herbs, darts from different places—it all depends on the reason I am making the doll. As you see from the illustration, the doll is holding a blade and a broom.

So this doll is made for protection and to sweep in blessings and good luck. A blade is worked with to cut something away or for protection. A broom can be worked with to sweep things in, sweep things out, or to do a cleansing on someone. It can also be worked with to keep folks out of your home. It all depends on the prayers and the actions that go along with the broom. These dolls are very special and, as far as I know, if there are other folks that make them, I don't know about it and I've not seen them.

A lot of the old folks are dying off, so their gifts and their knowledge are dying away with them. That's one of the reasons that I put these books out. I'm not gonna last forever, and as time goes on, folks are mixing and moxing and the work with everything but the kitchen sink and watering the work down until there's not gonna be anything left of this work.

I have always felt that dolls have a life of their own. They each have their own personality. They each have their own feel about them, so they have a life of their own, and I always pray over my dolls that I make that they find the right person, the person that they should be with. Yes, I sell the dolls, but my main purpose is not the money, it's the love of making the dolls and watching them come to life. It's being able to see them transform into a powerful thing.

All the dolls are made the same, but they always have their own personalities. They're always different in some kind of way. As we know, this work came out of slavery, and I call my dolls Big Mamas in honor of all the Big Mamas that were brought over here during slavery time and who took care of the slave owners' families. They were made to take care of someone else's children and work from sunup to sundown, yet they still found the strength to take care of their own families and to help their communities. The strength that it took just to make it through one day of life on the plantation just baffles me. I cannot even imagine what they had to endure. These women were strong and powerful in order to survive the horrors that they went through. They deserve to be honored and to be remembered.

I feel like their memory should be honored and I also feel like that dark time in America's history should never be forgotten, because to forget is to repeat. If you are a Conjure worker, you should be honoring the ancestors of this work. I have said this over and over and over again, because if it weren't for their suffering and their knowledge there would be no Conjure. The Big Mamas are my way of honoring them, of keeping their spirit alive. They deserve to be acknowledged, they deserve to be thought about, they deserve to have prayers said in their names, even though we don't know their names. If you are going to do this work, then you owe it to the folks that came before you, and what they went through should never be forgotten or sugarcoated.

For this work, any doll can be worked with. You don't have to have a homemade doll to load and work with; you can get a store-bought doll, take the head off of the dollie, and either fill the head with a packet or put the roots, herbs, and darts directly inside the body of the doll, then put the doll's head back on. I personally prefer to work with one of the Big Mama dolls that I've made or to simply work with a doll head (and I'm gonna talk about that later on in the book).

This work is gonna be a work of protection to protect your home or to protect yourself. You need the dirt from the four corners of your property, two needles with the eyes broken off of them bound together in a small cross, and a photo of your home or yourself, depending on what you're doing this for. (Most of the time, folks that live in an apartment won't work with the apartment building photo; they simply do a photo of themselves.) You also need a pinch of barberry root to bar your enemies, the dirt from a church, some lovage, and some angelica root. You're going to need five seven-day candles; white ones will work.

You are going to load the doll, then you are going to blow three breaths in the doll and put the head back on the doll. If you are going to put your ingredients in a packet, then you'll need a small piece of a white handkerchief to lay your roots, herbs, photos, and dirts in. You fold the handkerchief toward you into a small packet, then you bind everything together with red cotton string and you place the packet in the doll's head.

Once you have the doll put back together, it is time to place your doll in a candle setup. You put the first candle down, starting at the top, then you set the middle candle down, and then you set the bottom candle down, so they should all be in a line. These dolls can be made for many different conditions, but this one we're making for protection, so the next two candles are set down left to right because we are trying to nail down the protection that we're petitioning for.

You light your candles in the order that you laid them down in, and on each candle you're going to say your prayer and your petition. The prayer is a personal prayer because not everyone is going to need the same type of protection or want the same thing, so it's not a one-size-fits-all. I have found that the best way, when I'm doing a personal prayer, is to make it as short as possible. Repetition is everything, so write the prayer down so you can say the same prayer over each candle, each day that the candle burns.

When you have all your candles lit, then you need to say your prayer and petition at least three times during the day, preferably morning, noon, and night. If you can only do one of those times, I suggest that you do it at high noon when the sun is high in the sky.

That is a powerful time. If you can't then, just do the best that you can do. Don't stress over it. I will say this: Everything costs something. Nothing is free in this life. If you want success, you have to do the work. Spirit is not going to just let you do the minimum and bless you with the most. There're gonna be times when you don't wanna do the work; you're tired, you don't feel good, but hey, like my godfather Papa Hector Salva, author of *The 21 Divisions,* said, "Magic ain't free."

When you've done the work for the seven days, then it's time to test the power of the prayers that you've prayed into the doll, unless you have a strong discernment and you can feel the power of the doll. You need a pendulum, a glass of water, and a white stick candle. Set the doll up, place the candle on the left side of the doll and the glass of water on the right side. Say your prayers and petition the spirit that has now become your dollie to show you if the doll is full enough. If the pendulum moves slowly, then I would say you have to repeat the work. If you get good movement from the pendulum, then I would say that you did your job well and the dollie is full.

If you get a positive "yes" from the pendulum, then the next step is to find a place where the dollie wants to sit. Once again working with your pendulum, ask the questions of where the doll wants to sit. Once you get your answers, then you place the doll where it wants to be. This may sound strange to some folks but this is how it's done. Then, once a month you give your doll a candle and a cool glass of water, unless they ask for something else. Once a year refresh the work on your doll and you should have a protector for life if you did the work right.

Blue Bottles

Old Conjure workers have always worked with cobalt blue bottles. These special bottles are good for protection, locking things down, healing, and hiding your work. In the old days, the old timey Conjure doctors would treat their bottles with special roots and ingredients, then hang them in entries for a strong protection around their homes. If you walk into an old worker's home today and look behind the door, nine times out of ten you'll find a loaded blue bottle there.

You can do many different types of works with a blue bottle, but the most common types are protection and healing. The reason that the blue bottles are so powerful, or this is what I have been told growing up in the South, is that spirits cannot cross water. Blue, like the haint blue that a lot of the porch ceilings are painted with, makes spirit think that it's water. There is not a lot of information about working with blue bottles, but blue bottles like the medicine bottle make good containers for powerful Conjure work.

To Hide a Work

If you had a work that you were doing on a target and you knew, through discernment or some type of spiritual consultation, there was a chance that the target would find out about the work, you can hide that work in a blue bottle with other ingredients to keep the work from being detected. If you can find a blue medicine bottle, that works fabulously, because the opening is large. If you have to work with a blue bottle that is in the shape of a wine bottle, then you are going to have to make a packet that you can get into the mouth of that bottle.

This is why a medicine bottle works better, but when you have a job to do, you work with what you have.

You put your work together on the target, then you wrap it up tightly in a cloth packet. You put that packet into the blue bottle and then, in order to hide your work, you are going to add other ingredients into the blue bottle. This now becomes a double-action work. One, you got the target in there, and two, you're working with spirit and with that blue bottle to hide the work from the target. It may sound complicated, but it's not. It's really very simple.

After you put the packet into the bottle, then you load the bottle with a small pinch of slippery elm. Now, I was taught to work with slippery elm by small pinches because it can literally hide you from everything, which means you could be driving down the street and someone else in another vehicle could not see you and hit you, so be very careful with slippery elm. It takes just a small pinch. Then add some dirt dauber's nest, a pinch of red pepper (don't overdo it because you don't want the target so hotheaded that they can't be worked on), and you need a pinch of gunpowder. Fill the bottle up with some whiskey, put the seal on the bottle, and then you are going to place that bottle inside of a triangle setup of tea lights. You want to lock this work down, so you are going to do the setup with a tea light at the top, a tea light to the left, and a tea light to the right.

You are going to pray to the Holy Trinity that this work be hidden from the target and that the target be nailed down the same way Jesus was nailed on the cross, that the target not be able to move against you because their feet are nailed just like Jesus's feet were nailed to the cross. They cannot lift a hand to you because the right hand is nailed to the cross and the left hand is nailed to the cross, just like Jesus's hands were nailed to the cross. Repeat this work for twenty-one days and then put the bottle in a safe place.

Reversal Bottle Work

This work is done to reverse a cross condition back onto your enemies. You need a pen and paper, and you need to write a petition. Make a circle around the petition and put a cross inside of that circle. On the arms of the cross you are going to write the words "all my enemies." You need a thin rope in the center of which you've tied a knot loosely. Hold the rope in both hands and brush yourself down with that rope, petitioning spirit to bind all your enemies and to keep them away from you.

When you feel the time is right, pull the knot in the rope tight on the words "all my enemies." Be forceful with this. Wrap the rope around your petition and then place the petition paper into the bottle. To this, you are going to add a razor blade for protection, a closed safety pin for protection, some devil's shoestring to hobble the devil, some devil's bit for protection from the devil, some molasses to slow the devil down, and some angelica root to draw in the blessings.

Say your prayers and your petitions that you will be protected from your enemies and that all works that they have had their hands in against you will be reversed and returned to them. Fill the bottle with some whiskey, close the lid, and shake the bottle up as you say your prayer of protection and your prayer for the works that have been thrown at you to be reversed and to hit the target from whence they came.

You are going to need enough tea lights to make a circle around the bottle, plus four more. You are going to place them down in the opposite direction of the hands of the clock, or counterclockwise. As you lay each candle down, you petition spirit to reverse all works that have been sent to you by all your enemies, known and unknown. You're going to do this on each candle. Once you have that first circle laid down, then you are going to come back and inside of the reversal circle you are going to place a set of candles in the shape of a cross. So you will have a candle at the top of the bottle, you will have a candle at the bottom of the bottle, you will have a candle to the left of the bottle, and you will have a candle to the right of the bottle.

As you set each of those candles down, your prayer and your petition are going to be that you are protected against all enemies, known and unknown and any works that have been thrown at you are now reversed. As you light the reversal candles, that that energy will go back from whence it came. You are going to light the protection candles first in the same order that you set them down in. You are going to say the prayer over each candle as you light them.

The next step to this work is to light the reversal candles that were set up in the outer circle. These candles will also be lit in the direction that you set them up in. Over each candle you will pray to the spirit to reverse all works that have been sent against you and that those works be sent back from whence they came. This setup should be done for twenty-one days, three times a day, meaning you do the protection candles and prayers, and the reversal candles and prayers three times a day.

This is a triple action work. You have the bottle that in itself is a work, you have the protection work, and you also have the reversal work. You are doing three different things within one job; that is what makes this work a triple-action work. Once you have worked that bottle for twenty-one days, take your pendulum see how strong the bottle is. If you get a positive answer, then you put the bottle up and just keep it in a safe place.

This does not mean that your enemies can't ever throw at you again, but if you do this work right, it's gonna make them work harder to get to you and usually folks that do this type of thing to others get tired and give up. Just keep your cleansings up and work that bottle. It's not gonna last forever so you have to feed it with prayers and candles and shake it up in order to keep it working.

Bill Bowl

This work is to help you get your bills paid; that's why I call it the bill bowl. You will need

- a bowl
- a sheet of magnet
- a blue seven-day candle

I work with blue seven-day candles for money works and also for peaceful homework. This could be considered as a double-action work because if the bills are paid then there's not gonna be a lot of confusion, stress, and aggravation in the home. Most of the time trouble starts with worrying about money or cheating.

You need to take a three-day cleansing bath. That's one bath a day for three days. Pray the Isaiah 41 and the Psalm 23 either before, during, or after each bath. Then you need to take a fresh photo of yourself because now your spirit is cleansed. All that aggravation and everything should be washed away. You don't want that added to your work. Across the photo write in big letters, "All debts are paid!"

Place the photo in the bowl and cover it with the magnet. Place a copy of the bill you need to pay in the bowl on top of the magnet. You can only do one bill at a time. Once that bill is paid, you can take that bill out and add another one to the bowl if you need to pay more than one. Hold the blue candle up to your mouth and pray your petition into the wax, then set the candle on top of the bill and light it.

Take some change from your wallet and drop it into the bowl on top of the bill. In a strong, firm voice say, "I paid ________________ bill today!" Feed that bill daily with change out of your wallet and claim daily that that bill is paid. Once you have enough money to pay that bill, you can spend that change in the bowl on something you really need, then start on the next bill.

Don't worry about where the money's gonna come from or how you are going to gather the money to pay these bills. I'm a firm believer, and I was raised to believe, that the more you worry about money, the less you are going to have. You have to do the work and **know** that God is going to make a way for you. He gives us His word over and over again in the Bible that He will take care of us. We simply have to have faith. Do the work and let the spirits that walk with you do the rest.

Box Work

Box work is one of the better known works in Conjure. This type of work is usually done when you want to block someone, or when you are trying to hold someone or something down. Sometimes a protection box is also made by placing mirrors on the outside of the box, facing outward so they will deflect anything that is being thrown at you. These boxes should only be used in extreme circumstances when you feel you are truly being threatened. This is not the type of work that you should ever take lightly. I hesitated to add this type of work to the book, but a box is a container. If you feel like you need to have some strong protection, then this work may be able to help you.

Since working with boxes is work that everyone knows, I just want to put a short work here. I've done this work two different ways: I put the mirrors on the inside, and I put the mirrors on the outside of the box. It really just depends on if it matters to you how the box looks. If you want to hide the work then you put the mirrors on the inside of the box. If you don't care if people see that box and know that it's working there, then you can put the mirrors on the outside of the box. For this work, I'll give the recipe for a box work that I did with the mirrors on the inside of the box.

You need

- a nice box
- a photo of yourself
- some small mirrors
- frankincense
- myrrh
- bay leaves
- devil's bit

- devil's shoestring
- angelica root
- some dirt from the four corners of your home
- either a hot-glue gun or superglue

You also need Psalm 23. You can either print it out or you can tear it directly out of the Bible.

Fold Psalm 23 around your photo. Using two safety pins, pin Psalm 23 to your photo. Make the two safety pins in the sign of the cross, which means you pin one going one way and the other one going the other way so that they are crossing each other. As you are pinning Psalm 23 around the photo, claim God's protection and cover yourself with the blood of Jesus. I was raised to believe that the blood of Jesus is the greatest protection one can have, so when something harmful happens we were taught in church to say, "I cover myself with the blood of Jesus for protection." You can then either use a hot-glue gun or superglue to glue your mirrors facing outward inside your box. That means you will be looking at the backside of the mirrors.

Once all the mirrors are glued into the top and the bottom of the box, you then to need to add a layer of your roots and herbs into the bottom of the box. Lay your photo packet on top of the bed of herbs and roots. Hold the box up to your mouth and pray your prayers and petitions for protection from all enemies, known and unknown.

For this setup, because you are trying to lock down your protection, you are going to set the tea lights up top to bottom, left to right. Try to say your prayers for protection over the candles for as long as they are burning. Once your tea light set-up burns out, then add another layer of your roots and herbs on top of your packet. Hold the box up to your mouth again and pray your prayers and petition into the box. Call on the Holy Trinity and the ancestors for their protection. Once again cover yourself with the blood of Jesus. Close the lid on the box and then set the box in another tea light setup. Once the tea lights burn out, put your box up out of the reach of others.

You can also do this work to protect your money if you feel like someone is trying to cross your money up. All you have to do is add a five dollar bill from your wallet to the packet that you made with your photo and Psalm 23. To the ingredients you may want to add the ash from your business card or the name of your business. When doing a mirror work, you are deflecting any cross condition or works that are sent to destroy your prosperity.

The only limitations that we have in this work are the ones that we set on ourselves. This work was meant to be worked in order to keep the family unit safe, for safe travel, and to keep away cross conditions or from being hoodooed. There is no reason for anyone to have money issues that are caused by other folks. Don't set limitations on your success.

Bull Horn for Protection

The outside of the bull's horn protects the bone that is inside to keep the bull's horn safe. So why couldn't a horn be worked with for protection? If you don't have access to a cow head nowadays, you can find horns for sale online. If you are lucky and you get a fresh bull's horn, it takes a while to get it to dry out, but you can speed up the drying process by filling the horn full of rock salt. The rock salt will dry up all the moisture inside of the horn. You may have to change the salt out a few times before the horn is completely dry. Not only does the salt dry out the horn, but it also cleanses the horn because, as we know, salt cleanses.

Once you have your horn, to fix the horn you need to collect dirt from the four corners of your property. You also need to gather the dirt from the front door and the back door of your home. Take a photo of the family and burn it to ash, then you mix the ashes with the dirt you collected. You can add herbs to the other ingredients, such as angelica root for protection, Master of the Woods for power, lovage root for family love, lightning struck wood for strength, and Solomon's seal root for the wisdom to always know how to handle whatever comes your way. Mix all the ingredients together.

Once you get all your ingredients into the horn, you can close the end of the horn up. I personally like to stuff cotton into the end of the horn because cotton absorbs. Once you have the horn done, you can place it over the top of your doorway, beside your doorway, or on a shelf facing the door. It all depends on where you would like to place it in your home. Once a month, feed the horn some fire from a candle and some whiskey.

Money-Can Work

I love to work with cans! I have had an old coffee can for years and years. You can do all types of work in these cans. Nowadays, so many folks are in need. Most folks don't even have transportation, so think about that for a minute. Let it sink in. In this day and age, you would think everyone could afford a place to live, something to drive, and plenty of food to eat, but that's not the case. It seems to me instead of moving forward, we're actually moving backward in time.

I decided to share a work I have done in order to get me a new vehicle, but I have also done can work to get the home that I live in and have lived in for almost thirty-four years. This type of work really works. You have to stick with it; do not worry about where the money

is coming from. The car, the house, the bill being paid, where it's coming from—you have to know that it's coming.

If you need a vehicle, this work just may help you get one. Always be reasonable. If you can't afford $1,000 a month for a car payment, then do not get that type of car. Get something that you can afford. I can't guarantee this Money Can will get you a vehicle, but I can tell you I have gotten my last four this way. I personally don't pick the vehicle. I won't. I let spirit do it for me, and so far I've gotten lucky. I don't ask for a model year either, and every time I have needed to buy a car, I have found one newer than what I had to start with. This is just how I do it because I don't wanna set limits or miss a good deal because I wanted a brand-new vehicle. Either way, you work the can the same.

Get a large metal coffee can. Rinse it off with some cool running water and let it air dry. You need a sheet of candle wax, a magnet, and a photo of the car or truck you want. Like I said, please be reasonable and go for what you can afford. I like to burn a blue candle for this, but you can burn whatever you have. Place the photo in the bottom of the can and put the magnet on top of the photo. Pray over your candle and say your petition. Place the candle in the can and again claim your vehicle. Take some change from your wallet, drop it into the can, and say "I bought ____________________ today!"

Repeat this process every day and keep your candle going. Feed that can and claim that car or truck! This Money Can can be worked for all types of work, from buying a home to paying off large bills. All you have to do is feed the can and claim it! Have faith in God and God will bless you!

Loaded Blockbuster Candle

In this work you will need a large pillar candle. If you can find an orange one, then use orange. If you can't, then just use white. Take a pair of small scissors or a knife and dig a hole in either the bottom of the candle or the side of the candle. The reason you use scissors or a knife is because you are removing the blocks that are holding you back. Scoop wax from the hole. You need a plate to set your candle on. You need John 14 V 1-14, torn from an old Bible, your petition paper, and one small piece of High John root. Burn the Bible verse along with your petition. Mix this ash with a little powdered angelica root. Load your powder and the High John into the hole that you dug out, saving some to sprinkle on later. Fill the hole with the wax that you removed. Write your name on the candle along with the phrase: "I knocked and the door was open!"

Set the candle on the plate and sprinkle the leftover powder around the candle. Light the candle and pray that all blocks be removed. Take any leftover wax to a crossroads along with five pennies and leave it there.

Beeswax Reversal Candle

If you feel blocked or just feel like something is not right, you can do this little five-day reversal. You will need five pennies and five hand-rolled black beeswax candle sheets. Roll your candles away from you when you are making them. Do not add anything to these candles. Make sure you do this when the hands of the clock are moving downwards in order to remove.

While you are rolling the candles, call on God and Saint Peter to remove all blocks away from you. Once you have the candle rolled, take the candle and while praying to God and Saint Peter, wipe yourself off going downward from head to toe with the candle. Then take one of the pennies and wipe yourself down with the penny in the same fashion, going from the top of your head to the bottom of your feet. You then take that penny, turn it face down, and burn your candle on it. Once the candle has gone out, mash the leftover beeswax around the penny. Set the penny on the side of the plate and the next day repeat the instructions until you have burned all five candles.

On the sixth day, take the pennies and throw them in a crossroads away from your home. When you get home, light a white seven day vigil candle to God and Saint Peter and thank them for their help. This may seem like a really simple work, but I have had great results with this. There really is a whole lot of hocus-pocus to this work. It's usually simple and straight to the point, but the results are huge.

Coconut Work

The coconut makes a wonderful head for hitting a target. The coconut already has natural eyes and a mouth. There are a few old tricks that can be done working with a coconut. You don't hear of them much anymore. Here is a simple but effective one.

To Bring Him Back

I know some folks don't believe in this type of work, but like the old saying goes: You don't know what goes on behind closed doors and you don't know what happened to cause this separation for someone to leave home. Like I say, just because you know how to do something, doesn't mean you have to do it. If this work is not the type of work that you would want to do, then just keep it moving.

Get a small coconut and bore a hole in it. The easiest way to do this is where the eyes are. Doing it where the eyes are also kind of blinds the target, so they can't really see the work that you are doing. Drain the milk out and load the coconut with a photo of the target. To this add calamus, lovage, Master of the Woods, orange peel, and dirt from the front door stoop. Write your petition and add that into the coconut. Then you are going to baptize the coconut in the name of the target. This way the coconut represents the head of the target.

If you do this right, then the target should feel everything that the coconut feels. Set the coconut in a cross setup and pray over it while the candles are burning. Once the candles go out, get some red cotton string and start to cover the coconut by winding the string around the coconut.

The whole time you are wrapping the coconut, call out to the targets. Tonight, tell them they will get their behinds back home and stay home. They will be peaceful and loving. They will be happy at home. Make sure that you are wrapping the string toward you. On each wrap, make sure to say your petition. The petition is personal, so I'm not gonna give a set petition, because it differs from situation to situation. Just be very plain in your petition and get straight to the point. Make sure to write the petition down so you will be praying the same words over and over and over. Remember, words hold power.

Coconuts are also good for removing fussing and fighting out of the home. Go to the store and find a good-sized coconut. Bring it home and run some cool water over it. Call on the Trinity and the ancestors and ask them to remove whatever is in the house. Take the coconut and start at the back of your house. Using your left foot, gently kick the coconut through each room while praying that whatever is there is removed. Once you've gone through the whole house, take the coconut and throw it in the middle of the crossroads as hard as you can to break it. The goal is for the crossroads to soak up whatever is troubling your home.

You may want to do this work before you start to work with the coconut head. This way you know that anything that was in your home that was causing issues between y'all or any fussing and fighting that was stuck in the corners or on the walls is removed.

Conch Shell

We live in the water in our mothers' wombs for nine months before we are born. We are well protected within our watery home, safe and sound, being held in our mother's body.

The conch shell belongs to the mothers of the ocean. It has a living being housed in it, safe and sound and well protected. This is why it is good for protection work. This work can be left out in your home, and even the nosiest visitor won't know what is in that beautiful shell, since your protection work is for you and your loved ones. All they will see is a beautiful shell.

You need to get a large shell for this work. It is better if you can go to the beach and find one yourself. If you can't find one, then you can buy one and take it back to the ocean to bathe it in the healing protective waters of the mothers. You need

- a large shell
- a white hanky
- Psalm 23 taken out of the Bible
- an olive leaf
- bay leaf
- frankincense
- myrrh

a photo of the family
bloodroot
Master of the Woods

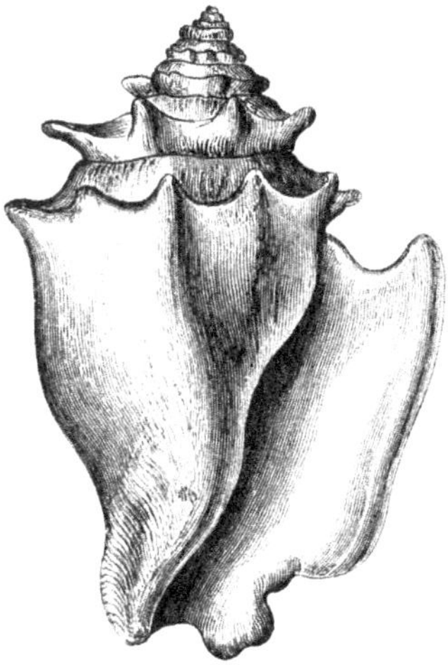

Cleanse your shell in the ocean waters and bring it home to air dry. These shells hold water, so it will still have some of the waters from the mothers of the ocean in it. Put the shell in a candle setup of five tea lights. Place one of the tea lights in the opening of the shell. The next step is to lay out your handkerchief. You will need another set of white tea lights for this step. Burn the Bible verse and the photo, place them in the center of the handkerchief, then pray your petition and Psalm 23 over each of the other ingredients and place them on the hanky.

Place the tea lights in the cross setup with one sitting on top of your ingredients. Pray over your work again and light the tea lights in the order that you set them down in. Go as often as possible and pray over the ingredients as the candles are burning. Once the candles have burned out, you'll fold your hanky in half coming toward you. You should have what looks like a hanky sausage. Hold the hanky by each end and tie it into a loose knot. Pray your prayer and petitions into the handkerchief. Then, right before you are finished, pull the handkerchief tight. This will tighten the knot up and close the ingredients inside the handkerchief. Hold the hanky up to your mouth and pray your petition and your prayer into the handkerchief. Feed the hanky, which has now become a packet, with a little bit of whiskey.

Set the hanky in another five sets of tea lights, then repeat your prayers and petitions at least three times while the setup is burning. Once the candles have burned out, take the packet and place it inside the shell. Then hold the shell up to your mouth and repeat your prayers and petitions three times. Then you dress the shell with a little bit of the all the ingredients you used to feed the packet and a couple of drops of whiskey.

Set the complete work in a tea light setup of five tea lights, place the tea lights in the shape of a crossroads, and put the fifth tea light on the curve of the shell. Light the tea lights and repeat your prayers and petitions. Be very mindful of fire; make sure that you watch your work. Every type of candle is very flammable. Do not leave this or any other work alone with the candles burning.

Once the tea lights have burned out, place the shell in a safe place up high. Once a week feed this shell and burn a set of tea lights. This will keep your work alive.

Conjure Balls

Conjure balls can be made with wax, clay, or mud from a crawdad mound. They can be made to draw prosperity, to draw love, for domination work, or they can also be worked for darker works. These balls fall under the category of a container because the ball is built around the work.

Most old workers will say that the ball is the head of the target. The crown of our head is one of the most important parts on our bodies that can be hit hard when an enemy tries to throw at us. The Conch Shell work above was done for those who had to be protected.

The target's personal items are placed in the Conjure ball along with a verse from the Bible. It is all burned to ash. All of this is mixed with the clay to make the target's head. Period. Of course, while the ball is being made, you are very focused on the target and you are praying the whole time in their name.

In order to do this, you need a photo of the target, you need some dirt from the front and back doors of their home, and you need their handwritten petition of what it is that they want to happen. Then, from that petition, you will add a list of ingredients to go with the condition that you are working on for them.

These balls may seem simple, but they're powerful, and you have to remember that they are built by a living thing, which adds more to the power of the work. If you think about it, that's a lot of work for that little crawdad to bring that dirt up out of that ground to make the mound. This work can be made to fit any type of situation that you come across: protection, domination, even crossing work or to slow the enemy down.

I wanted to add this to the Conjure ball section. I was asked not too long ago by one of my students if you can work more than one target in one ball. We were talking about clay balls. If you were working on three targets that are dealing with the same situation, you can add all three of them to the work. The way you do that is that you make three small balls with their photos burnt to ash. Say your prayers and petition over each one of them, what you want the target to do, and then you roll it into a very small ball. Once you have those mini balls made, then you can squash the three of them together, but don't mix them up. You build your main ball around that.

Once you have all three of them enclosed, then you dry the clay or mud or whatever you made the ball out of, just like you would a regular Conjure ball. Then you work that ball just like you would any other ball, except when you are calling the name of the target out, you will actually call all three names out, because they are all three combined in that one work. Doing the targets in three separate small balls also separates them, so if they're causing issues together, this is gonna help to pull them apart. If it is for a different type of condition, and it was dealing with three separate things, then you wouldn't be able to do it like that.

Glass Protection Ball

If there ever comes a time when you need to erect a strong wall of protection, get a clear glass ornament ball (one that has a hole or opening in it) and then make a wash of equal parts of frankincense, of pinch of cayenne pepper, master root to give you the upper hand; calamus root, and lemon juice to cut the negative conditions. Add a pinch of gunpowder to the wash to heat up your work, with a dash of whiskey to feed the spirits. Make sure you pray over your work from start to finish.

Wash the outside of the glass ball with the wash while praying your petition. Let the ball air dry in a candle setup of tea lights. Once the ball is dry, place the photo or petition of the person or situation needing protection inside the glass ball with frankincense, calamus, dragon's blood, and dirt from a stop sign. You work with the dirt from the stop sign to bring all the troubles to a dead stop. You need an open safety pin to keep your roads open and a pinch of sulfur to run the devils off.

After you load the glass ball with your ingredients, hold the ball up close to your mouth and pray your petition three times in the name of the Holy Trinity and the ancestors. Then close the opening on the ball and place it in the candle setup. Hang the ball in a window facing the east. Refresh the ball once a week in the candle setup.

Conjure Bag

Conjure bags are one of the best-known works in Conjure. Everyone knows how to make these bags, it seems. Some folks call these bags mojo bags, Conjure bags, or Conjure hands. I personally prefer a packet to a Conjure bag, the reason being that the packet is much smaller. Even though it is smaller, it does the same job that the larger Conjure bags do. These bags can be made for anything from luck to love.

I am not gonna write a lot about it. I'm just going to give a couple of recipes for those who may not have a good Conjure bag recipe. The important thing about these bags is to remember to keep them close to your body and to feed them in a candle setup and with some whiskey once a week to keep them alive. If you do these things, then your bag should work well for a long time. Remember to breathe your prayer into your bag and to set the bag in a crossroad setup of candles once you have the bag made. This will add life to your bag and add power. Below you will find a couple of recipes for my favorite Conjure bags. I know they work and have worked well for me.

Love Conjure Bag

lovage root to promote love
damiana for love
a strong magnet to draw
olive leaf for protection
calamus root to be in control
orange peel to draw

Add the photos and petitions for the bag.

Money Conjure Bag

a magnet
money from your wallet
five finger grass
dirt from a crossroads
dirt from your front and back doors
hair from the crown of your head
Psalm 23

Add all the ingredients into the bag and follow the instructions for the setup.

Conjure Hand

A Conjure hand is nothing more than a smaller version of a Conjure bag. To make a Conjure hand, you need

- a three-by-three piece of red flannel
- a needle
- red cotton thread
- five tea lights for your candle setup
- the ingredients you will be laying down on the flannel

Lay your red flannel out on the table, then place all your ingredients in the center of the square. Fold the flannel toward you, turn it and fold it again, then fold each end. Using your needle and thread, whipstitch the hand closed, then, depending on what the hand is for, you wrap the hand tightly with red cotton string. Make sure that on each whipstitch you say your petition. As you're wrapping it with the red cotton string, you will also say your petition and your prayers.

Once the Conjure hand is made, you feed it some whiskey. Hold it up to your mouth and pray your petition and prayers into the hand, then place the hand in a candle setup and burn the candles on directly on the hand. Once the candles have burned out, then the hand is ready to carry. Make sure you feed your hand at least once a week. I'm going to add a couple of recipes below.

Protection Hand

Here is a recipe for a packet that will protect you from being conjured.

saltpeter: 1 pinch
angelica root: 1 pinch
dirt dauber's nest: 3 pinches
crab shell: 1 pinch
bay leaf: 1 pinch
the heads of three matches

As you add a pinch of each of the ingredients, you say: "I'm covered from the top of my head to the bottom of my feet by the blood of Jesus." And then you simply sew your packet. Repeat the prayer as you're sewing each stitch and as you are wrapping the packet.

Domination Hand

For this hand, you need a photo of the target who will be dominated and the following ingredients.

calamus root
licorice root
dirt dauber's nest
a pinch of graveyard dirt (If you do not know how to collect graveyard dirt, then do not make this hand, or just take it out. The graveyard is nowhere to be if you don't know what you are doing.)
Master of the Woods
If you can, get a sock of the target. It actually works better when you are trying to dominate someone. If you can't, then just work with the red flannel.

As you are adding each ingredient onto your red flannel, call the target's name out and demand that they do whatever it is that you want them to do. Just remember that any work that can be done can be undone. Make sure that you are well protected and don't end up being the one that is dominated. Once again, I remind y'all that just because you know how to do something doesn't mean you have to do it.

Crab Shell

When you are working with animal parts you should always look at the way the animal acts, how they move. Get to know the animal and how they can be worked with in magic. The crab is a good example. The pinchers can be worked with to hold things down, and the shell could be worked with for protection. The crab can move frontward and backward, so it can be worked with for confusion types of works and also reversal works.

To stop an enemy you need a crab claw and some red thread. Take a photo of the enemy, X out the eyes and mouth, fold the photo in half, and place in the crab claw while saying your prayers and petition. Then take the red thread and bind the claw up. Say your prayer as you are wrapping the claw. Once it is finished you can place it in a box or somewhere safe.

D

Deer Toe Pocket Piece

I don't know what it is about animal parts that have me so attracted to them. It could be because I'm a bone reader and I'm just naturally drawn to them. The trick with reading the bones or working with any part of an animal is understanding the traits of that animal, understanding how the animal lives and survives in the wild.

I know some of you may be thinking, "What in the world does the deer toe have to do with protection?" The answer to this question is to think about the deer; a deer can hide from a hunter in plain sight. They are also very good at standing still, but when they have to run, they can get to moving around. They are fast on their feet.

If you are trying to protect yourself from a known or unknown enemy, then you can load the work in the deer toe and be well protected. Not only does the toe hold the essence of the deer, but it is also hard as a rock. This work can also be done as a pocket piece because the dear toe is small enough so you can carry it in your pocket, or the ladies can carry it in their undergarments.

This packet may seem small but it really does pack a punch. You can do this work for protection, prosperity, Essence of Bend Over, it can even be done for Shut Your Mouth types of work. You may be thinking, "How would using a deer toe to do Shut Your Mouth work?" The answer is simple. If you work with or you are around the target daily, then this is a good pocket piece for you to carry. You can make the piece in the name of the target and carry it in your pocket. When you're around the target, hold the piece in your hand while you're praying your petition that they shut up and move on.

I'm going to give you the basic instructions for putting together your own deer toe pocket piece. Since the deer toe is naturally hollow, it makes a perfect container. Gather all your ingredients for this work. I usually work with three or four ingredients because of the size of the deer toe. I burn the photographs and the petitions to ash, then I mix the ash with the herbs and roots that I am going to be working with. Before you start your work, make sure that you wash the deer toe with some cool running water and let it air dry. Using tea lights, place the deer toe in a cross setup.

Petition the spirit of the deer that the toe came from. Ask that the spirit feed the pocket piece with the power of protection. Let the candles burn out, then you are going to repeat the process with the roots and herbs that you have chosen to load into the pocket piece. Make sure to say your prayers over the ingredients at least three times. Once this is done it's time to load the herbs, roots, and ash into the deer toe. You can seal the hole in the toe by using either melted wax or self-hardening clay. If you are really gifted, you could even put beadwork around the top.

Once you have everything together and the toe is loaded and sealed, then it is time to place it in another candle setup. This needs to be done at least three days in a row. You can work with your pendulum to make sure that the pocket piece is filled with power. Once it is ready, you can dress it with a little bit of whiskey to feed it. Then you carry the piece in your pocket. These are just the basic instructions so you can make any type of pocket piece that you need. You just follow these simple instructions. The ingredients that you are working with should fit the target or the reason you are making the pocket piece.

Dollies

When you are trying to make someone do what you want them to do, the best way is to make a doll of them. The dolls can be made from clothing that the target has worn or they can be made with red flannel. Of course, the clothing that they have worn is gonna have soaked up their essence, so it would be better to make the dollie out of that. When you are trying to nail someone down, a sock is the way to go to put the dollie together.

To load the dollie, you will need some cotton. The reason cotton is worked with is because cotton absorbs and holds onto stuff. If you have ever dipped a cotton ball in liquid, you know the cotton ball soaks up the liquid, making it perfect to stuff a doll with. To make the doll, you need to cut out a pattern for the dollie. The little gingerbread patterns work best. Once you have the dollie cut out of whatever material you choose to work with, you need to have some red cotton string and a sharp sewing needle so you can sew the doll up.

The first thing you do is to make three knots. On the first knot you say, "In the name of God the Father." The next knot you say, "In the name of God the Son." And on the last knot, "In the name of the Holy Spirit." Then you can either whipstitch or regular stitch the doll together. Either way you choose to sew the doll up, you are going to pray over each stitch. You call the target's name and you say what it is that you want to happen. When I sew a doll, I like to start on one side of the head to the feet, then back up to the other side. I'll leave the top of the head open so it will be easier for me to stuff the doll.

I'm going to give you a work that can be worked on when you have an unruly child that doesn't want to listen. You are going to make two dolls for this, one for the child and, yes, one for you.

To the child's doll, you will add allheal, lovage root, bloodroot, calamus root, mother's wart, lavender, and dirt dauber's nest. As you are putting all the ingredients into the doll, you are praying over each ingredient. Pray your petition. Each situation is different and each child is different so you have to decide what your prayer and your petition is. Place a photo in the head of the dollie of the child. Once you have the doll named and blessed, speak to the doll as you would your child and tell the doll what it is you want the child to do. You can add whatever roots and herbs that you choose to the doll; these are just ones that I work with. You can also add those roots and herbs to an oil and make a dressing oil to dress the doll.

I'm not gonna tell you what to add to your dollie but I would suggest that you add things like allheal, bloodroot, lovage root, lavender, and maybe some roses to fully pull forth love. I'll leave that up to you; these are just some suggestions. You're a grown-up; you should know what you need to help pull your child closer. When you have the dollies ready, tie your child's doll to a blue pillar candle and your doll to a white candle. Place your candle at one end of the table and your child's candle at the other end. Light your candle and say your prayer and petition over it, then light your child's candle and say your prayer and petition over that candle. Move your child's candle a little closer, about five inches, as you repeat your prayers and your petitions three times. Then move your child's candle daily, about five inches, at the hours of 6:00 a.m., noon, and 6:00 p.m. Each time you move the candle, you will pray your petitions and prayers over the candle. Continue moving your child's candle until it is right up on your candle. Once the two candles are touching, take a red ribbon and tie them together. Tie three knots. On each knot say your prayer. End each prayer with the name of God the Father, God the Son, and God the Holy Spirit, then repeat your petition again.

This is a good work to do when there is a lot of fussing and fighting between a parent and a child. By placing the child's candle away from you then drawing it back, it pulls the child's spirit closer to the parent. Depending on your child's personality and the power of their will, you may have to repeat this work. Once the candles have burned out, remove the dolls from the candle glass jars, tie the ribbon back around them, then wrap the dollies in a white handkerchief and place them in a safe place. I would do this at least once a month to make sure that everything is running smoothly.

Egg Container Works

Eggs are powerful containers because an egg will hold on to any condition, positive or negative. Most folks know about working the egg to remove blocks and cross conditions, but the egg is a powerhouse when it comes to containers. The egg is worked with a lot more than just in cleansing work. Eggs can be used to draw things to you or remove them. They can also be used to slow something down, because once you lock something down in an egg, it is trapped. This applies to money, love, prosperity, success, and even what some folks call darker works.

Nailing an Enemy Down

Here is a simple egg working to slow down an enemy who just will not leave you alone. One of the reasons that eggs are so powerful is because the egg can hatch a living thing. When a hen sits on her eggs, they turn into baby chicks, so in all reality the egg is a living thing. For this work, you need to poke a hole in a brown egg and drain out the yolk and the egg white. Then you need a photo of your enemy, and one of those small gold safety pins, one of the tiny ones. Say your prayer and petition over the photo, then fold the photo away from you and pin it closed with the small safety pin. Place the photo in the small pin inside the egg, then place a pinch of red pepper, a pinch of slippery elm in order to hide the work, a pinch of dirt from a stop sign, a pinch of dirt dauber's nest, calamus root, and grains of paradise.

Melt some wax in a double boiler. You will use this wax to close up the egg. If you can get a pinch of gunpowder and add it to the egg, it will make the work stronger. I know nowadays it's hard to get gunpowder, but one way that you can get it is by buying fireworks and taking some of the ingredients out of them in order to do your work. Before you close the egg up with your wax, you need to petition God and your ancestors to bring forth justice upon this enemy. Once it's closed, you will also need to place the egg into a cross candle setup. You then need to work the egg in the cross setup for three days. Now, at this time, you can either throw the egg into running water or bury it away from your home, but if you really wanted to kick the work up a notch, you could bury the egg in a flowerpot and plant ivy on top of it.

Planting the egg in a pot is special and it also is a hidden work. Depending on why you're doing it, the target could walk right by the work and never even know that it was there. As the plant grows, so will the work grow stronger. You just have to remember that you have to take care of the plant if you bury any type of work in a container and place a plant over it. If the plant dies, the work dies. So if you decide to plant this work, where would you place the plant? You have to remember that wherever you place the pot, that's where the work's going. So if you're trying to slow somebody down, we know that things do not grow well in the north, so you would need a hardy plant in the planter, and place it in the north. If you wanted to remove them away from you then you would place the planter somewhere facing the west, because we know that the sun goes down in the west. It's really up to you whatever you decide to do with the egg, but just know that the longer you work the egg, the stronger the work will become.

Blockbuster Egg Trick

For this work you will use the egg to catch those blocks keeping you in a bind and remove yourself out of the situation. Poke a hole in an egg and let the yolk and the white drain out of the egg. Rinse the inside of the egg with some warm soapy water. If you want to kick this trick up a notch and make it a triple-action job, make a cleansing wash with your herbs and roots, then wash the egg inside and out while saying your prayers for all roads to be open and that you may have total success. For the cleansing wash you can use frankincense, calamus root, angelica root, lemon, and five finger grass. Some of these herbs do more than one job, which will pack your work with more power.

You will also need dirt or a small stone from the four corners of a crossroads. Let the egg dry by placing the egg, your photo, and all the other ingredients for this work in a circle setup of tea lights. The heat from the tea lights will help heat up the work, therefore drying the egg and adding more power. You have to also remember that a circle is a never-ending thing. You can't get in it and you can't get out of it.

Once the egg is dry, you can load in the ingredients. You will need your dirt or small stone from the four corners of the crossroads, your photo burnt to ash, a small piece of magnet, licorice root for power, and Master of the Woods. Hold the egg close to your mouth and say Psalm 23 V 1, "The Lord is my shepherd; I shall not want." You need to say this in a firm, strong voice. That's God's promise to us that we should never want for anything in our life. You say the prayer three times along with your petition, then you're going to blow three puffs of tobacco smoke into the egg while saying your name. Then you stick a piece of tape over the hole to hold the smoke and the ingredients in. Now the egg is ready to be put to work.

You can work the egg as a cleansing tool to brush yourself down from head to toe, or you can work the egg when you feel like you have blocks. To work the egg to cleanse yourself off, you start at the crown of your head and you wipe yourself down with the egg, going in a downward motion until you reach your feet. You should clean your feet with the egg going from heel to toe. Make sure you cleanse your head, your neck and shoulders, and feet thoroughly. These are the areas where we hold cross conditions the most. Cleanse yourself until the egg feels full, then repeat the same procedure with the four white tea lights. Wipe yourself from head to toe with the tea lights while praying to remove all blocks. Place the tea lights in a cross setup with the egg sitting in the middle of them. Light the candles from top to bottom and right to left and let them burn out.

For the next four days you will repeat the same cleansing technique with the egg and the four new candles, for a total of five days. Five is the number of the crossroads. When the five days are up, you will go and throw the egg in the center of the crossroads. Throw it hard enough so that eggshell breaks. Say your petition and prayer for your roads to be open. The egg traps the blocks that have been put on you. When you bust the egg open, you are busting yourself out of the situation that has kept you bound down.

Normally, when I do blockbuster type of work, I use a medicine bottle or a glass vigil, but I chose an egg for this work to show you that when you break that egg open at the crossroads, you are opening your own roads. This work is simple; it takes a little time but it gets the job done. We also have to remember: Whatever our eyes see, our mind believes. So throwing that egg in the center of that road and watching it bust open is planting a seed in our mind that our roads are now open, which will change the way that we think about the issue that we were having. Visuals are always good with this work because they plant that seed. The old folks say when a seed is planted, a tree will grow.

Fish

Animal parts have long been worked with in Conjure. Back in the days of the ancestors, they worked with whatever they had. You catch the fish, you clean the fish, you have to gut the fish, but then what do you do with the insides of the fish? Most of the times, or at least I'm speaking for my family, they would cook the fish with the fish head on so even the head did not go to waste, but the insides is a whole 'nother story.

When you're working with animal parts, it's important to know that animal's habits, what the animal does in its daily life, and what the animal likes. If you were trying to get rid of somebody and to move them away from you, you could get one of their dirty garments (socks work best, but whatever you can get) and make a packet out of that by working with those fish insides. Since you have a dirty garment that the target has worn, that's just like having the target's photo, because that garment now holds the sweat and the energy from their body. The dirty garment has picked it up.

Socks are really best for this because all you have to do is load the fish guts into the sock and bind it with some red cotton string. Make three knots with the string in the name of God the Father, in the name of God the Son, and in the name of God the Holy Spirit.

We hear a lot of talk about running water when talking about getting people away from you. So what better way to remove someone from your life than working with the insides of a fish? Where do fish live? The water! Not only that, but by working with the insides of the fish, as those insides rot, the target is also going to feel the effects of that rot.

I know that there are some folks who feel like this type of work is wrong, but if someone does something so horrible to you that you want to remove them out of your life, what does it matter what spirit does to them? Spirit is always going to get justice for you, no matter what type of work you're doing. If you're calling for justice, it is out of your hands. So the best way to know that this type of work is the right thing to do is to do divination on the target to see if you should even be working on them at all, or if spirit has got everything handled. You and you alone are responsible for the works that you do, and once you offer that work up to spirit, it is out of your hands. There're no take backs, so make sure that the works you do are justified.

G

Gloves

I have never shared this work with folks before, outside of my in-house students or clients. I think it is safe to say that since this is one of my own personal works, it is not a well-known work. Gloves are powerful tools to work with because they represent the hands—hands that can offer a raise, pay a bill, be stopped from causing harm, and be uplifting.

I wasn't gonna place this working here, lest it be used against me, but then I thought, "Why not?" I'm well protected. The idea behind this work is to hold the target in the palm of your hand. You know the old saying, "I got them eating out of the palm of my hand?" This work is meant to work the same way.

The first work I want to share is what I call a Pay Me Hand. This work is done when there is money that is owed to you and the target hasn't kept their word to pay you back. I have found that this hand is very powerful if you tie the glove to a seven-day candle.

Pay Me Hand

You need a set of cloth gloves, the target's photo, five tea lights, and one purple or orange seven-day candle. The first step is to make a wash with calamus, licorice, and Master of the Woods. Once the wash is made, put the gloves in the wash while you pray your petition over them. Once they have soaked up the wash, lay them out to dry.

Once the gloves are dry, lay one of them out with the palm up. Place the photo of the target in the palm of the glove and add a magnet, five finger grass, and the herbs from the wash. Then place the palm of the other glove on top of it and either pin them together or nail them together. Place the hand in a five tea light setup. Pray your petition and prayers over the setup while they burn.

When the setup burns out, tie the hand around the seven-day candle. Try to say your prayers and petition over the hand at least three times a day. You need to keep the heat going on the target until you get your money. Once the money is paid back, let the target go, cleanse your gloves with a wash of table-salt water, let them dry, and put them up until you need them again.

Money in the Hand

This work is done to draw money into the palms of your hands. We all need an extra helping hand sometimes. All things are possible with faith and a little work. The only thing that can stop you from having what you want and need in your life is you. You can also work the gloves to draw a home, a car, a job, or whatever it is that you're looking for into your life.

If you want a new car, place a photo of the car in the palm of the glove, then add a magnet. On top of that, add some Master of the Woods, Solomon's seal for wisdom, orange peel to draw, and bay leaf for good luck. Then you simply follow the instructions from the Pay Me Hand. The only difference is that this Money in the Hand work is put up until you get what you're asking for. You should work this work at least once a week to pull in what you're asking for.

Gourds

I like gourds for Conjure work because they shake things up. This makes them powerful for cleansing work. They are also good for protection work because they are hard to break. Gourds can be used in many different kinds of container work.

Shake the Devil Off Protection Rattle

You can make a protection rattle with a gourd that will do a few different things. The rattle will be linked to your spirit because you load your personal items into the gourd. The gourd will represent your head. Then, when you cleanse yourself with the gourd by shaking it from the crown of your head to the bottom of your feet, you will be shaking off all the cross conditions. Whoever is trying to put you in a fix won't have an easy time, because as soon as you feel work is being done on you, it will be shaken off, like the gospel song "Shake the Devil Off" (read below) for the petition in this work.

Here's how to make your own gourd rattler. Drill a hole in the gourd. Gather four small pebbles from each corner of a crossroads. You need a magnet to pull off all cross conditions. You need some dragon's blood, bloodroot (bloodroot represents the blood of Jesus and the blood of our ancestors), a pinch of devil's claw (to scratch away the devil when he's riding your back), dirt from your footsteps (each time you shake the gourd rattler, your enemies will get confused because they won't find your footsteps to play their dirty tricks; remember you have to be tricky in this work), some seashells (because the ocean is a powerful cleanser), and the ash from a burned photo of you. You also need angelica root, frankincense, Master of the Woods to give you the upper hand, and a pinch of sulfur because sulfur kills tricks and runs the devil off.

Don't get heavy-handed with the ingredients when you load the gourd, because you want it to shake right. Once you have the gourd ready, hold the open gourd to your mouth, state your full name and your petition over the gourd three times, and then seal the gourd shut. If you want to go an extra step, you can paint eyes, a nose, and a mouth on the gourd using paints that have been loaded with burnt ash from your photo. This links your spirit to the work and it will also fool a worker who is trying to throw at you, because they won't be able to tell the difference because you are also part of the gourd.

Place the rattle in a cross candle setup. Light the candles from top to bottom and right to left. Petition God and your ancestors to fill the gourd rattler with their power. Cover the rattler with the blood of Jesus and ask spirit to shake off all the devils in your life. Repeat this layout for five days.

Below you will find my rendition of the hymn "Shake the Devil Off." This will add power to your own prayers and petitions. When you feel overloaded with cross conditions, hold the gourd rattler to the crown of your head and wipe yourself downward to your feet. As you wipe yourself with the rattler from the crown of your head all the way to the soles of your feet, shake it as hard as you can. Tell the devil in your life they are covered with the blood of Jesus and demand they get moving around. Don't forget to swipe those feet. When you feel you have cleansed yourself well, place the rattler in a cross setup. This work might be long, but it will send the devil running for the hills.

I shake the devil off

I cover myself with the blood of Jesus, I shake the devil off

he won't be driving this whip, I shake the devil off

In the name of Jesus, I shake the devil off

shake shake shake

I shake the devil off my back

shake shake shake

I cover him with the blood of Jesus

shake shake shake

I shake the devil off!

H

Handkerchief

Stop a Bill Collector

Spread out a white handkerchief flat on the table. Draw a circle in the center with a permanent black marker. Inside the circle, make a cross. Write the bill collector's name on the arms of the cross. Tear Proverbs 22 V 27 ("If thou hast nothing to pay, why should he take away thy bed from under thee?) out of the Bible and place it in the center. Then put the dirt from the four corners of your property, dirt from the post office, alum, and a pinch of sulfur in the center of the circle. Fold the handkerchief in half, folding it away from you, then start rolling the handkerchief away from you until it looks like a tube. As you are rolling the handkerchief away from you, call on Moses. Petition Moses to help you in your time of need. Tell him you're being harassed by these folks, that they won't let you rest. Explain to him that you are doing your best. You can just talk to him and ask him to stop them.

Get a blue candle and write the collector's name in the wax, then make a hole in the candle and put a small pinch of alum in the hole. Say your prayers, then light the candle. Pick up the handkerchief and fix it in a loose knot. Hold one end in each hand. Start praying. Ask that these folks leave you alone. When you feel the spirit on you strong, in a loud voice demand they leave you be. Pull the knot in the handkerchief as tight as you can. Then you wrap the packet around the base of the candle. You need to pray over this at least three times a day when the hands of the clock are going downward. Pray your petition three times each time. Repeat the candle and the prayers until the collectors leave you alone, then you can take the packet to running water and throw it in.

Make 'Em Act Right

Over the years I have done a lot of work for clients and their jobs. It seems that in every job, there is at least one person that you have to contend with, who always keeps a mess going, or always feel like they run things. Of course, you could just hotfoot them, but then their family would be affected too for their wrongdoing, and you can't just go around hotfooting folks. You have to make sure that it is justified work, and not only that, you have to be sure that you really understand what hotfoot work does. In my opinion, and this is just my opinion, folks use hotfoot works too often when there are other things that could be done to right a bad situation other than hotfoot. I was taught as a young worker that hotfoot should only be done when everything else has failed. This type of work is serious work and it should never be done lightly. It's also dangerous, because once the work is done, it's out of your hands, and you don't know what the person that you hotfooted is going to go through. The justice in a work should also be rightful for the crime.

Some folks deserve this type of work, but most don't. There are other things that can be done to resolve a situation, and here is one. Spread out a white handkerchief flat on the table. In the center of the handkerchief, draw a circle with a permanent black marker. Inside the circle draw the arms of a cross. From the Bible, tear out Joshua 1 V 8 and place it in the center of the handkerchief. Run two sewing needles through the verse in the sign of a cross.

Here's the verse:

> This book of the law shall not depart out of thy mouth; but thou shalt meditate therein day and night, that thou mayest observe to do according to all that is written therein: for then thou shalt make thy way prosperous, and then thou shalt have good success.

This verse is telling them to follow God's law, and only then will they prosper. If they are causing trouble for you on the job, then they are not following God's law and they will not prosper from it. Place a pinch of powdered sugar and Master of the Woods on top of the Bible verse. Fold the handkerchief in half coming toward you and then roll it toward you. Dress a purple candle with Bend Over oil and write the person's name around the wick. Hold the candle up close to your mouth and pray over it. Light the candle.

Pick up the handkerchief and fix it in a loose knot. Hold one end with each hand. Start praying. Ask for peace, and ask that the person causing the issue start to act right and stop causing problems. When you feel the spirit on you strong, in a loud, demanding voice demand they leave you alone and let you have peace. When you feel the time is right, pull the knot as tight as you can. Wrap the packet around the base of the candle three times a day when the hand is going upward on the clock. Make sure you pray your petition three times over the candle. Repeat the candle and the prayers until you have the peace that you are looking for.

Here's one more: I have done a lot of this work for husbands who can't seem to control their wanderlust and keep their behinds at home. Spread out a white handkerchief flat on a table. Using a permanent marker, in the center write, "What God has joined, let no man put asunder." Take a chapter and verse from the Song of Solomon that you feel drawn to and place it on the handkerchief, then take a photo of you and your husband when y'all were happy. Fold the photo where y'all are facing each other. Lay the photo on the handkerchief. Fold the handkerchief in half coming toward you, then roll it the rest of the way coming toward you. Pray the whole time that you are rolling that handkerchief toward you, because you're bringing your loved one back to you.

Once again, you fix the handkerchief in a loose knot and you continue to pray. When you feel the time is right, you pull that handkerchief as tight as you can. Hold the handkerchief up to your mouth and continue to pray over it. When you feel the power in the handkerchief, then dress four tea lights and set them up in the sign of the cross. Set the handkerchief in the center of the setup and let the tea lights burn out. Do this for three days. When the three days are up, place the packet under his side of the mattress.

I

Ice Trays

I think that almost everybody in the world knows about freezing a target, where you put them in a container and you put them in the freezer to chill them out, settle them down, and freeze them in the position that they're in, but I have not seen anyone write about working with ice trays. The good thing about the ice tray is that it has many different slots to it, so you don't have to have all these different kinds of containers in your freezer. You simply need an ice tray.

There's more to freezer work than putting the enemy in the freezer. Yes, it works, and yes, it needs to be done at times, but you can also freeze the trauma and drama that are going on in your home. The ice tray is great for this type of work. Not everybody in the home cuts up, but you can sweeten your home by dedicating a single ice tray to your home and working that ice tray to bring peace and happiness into your home.

The first step is to cleanse the house, then do some protection work and some road-opening work. You don't want to freeze any ongoing issues. Load each slot with a photo of the home and a photo of each person in the home, then add these ingredient: a pinch of sugar (to sweeten), a pinch of lavender (for peace), and a pinch of devil's bit (to keep the devil out). Then you can either fill each slot with water or you can make the wash below and add it to the tray. Use only the slots needed for this work; save the other ones in case something comes up. Once you have the tray ready, then you place it in the freezer.

Ice Tray Wash

angelica root
devil's claw
master root
orange peel
bay leaf
basil
lemon balm

Add all the ingredients to a pot of water. Bring the water to a boil, then turn the fire off and steep the wash. Once the wash has cooled, you can strain the roots and herbs out of the wash, and then fill your ice tray up with the wash and place it in the freezer. You can save the rest of the wash and add it to your mop water, or you can clean your door stoop with it and sprinkle the leftover roots and herbs around the door stoop.

Jars

General Instruction on Working a Jar

This is general instruction on how to work a Conjure jar. What goes into the jar depends on why the jar is being made. Once you get the jar made, it's important that you burn a candle of some type on top of the jar. Some folks like to burn stick candles but to me that makes too much of a mess on top of the jar. I personally prefer tea lights. Nowadays, you can get tea lights in any type of color you're looking for. Once you have all the ingredients within the jar and have said your prayers and your petitions into the jar and closed the jar up, you need to shake the jar vigorously. This keeps the ingredients moving around and working. If you just let the jar sit there, the work is going to become stagnated and it's not gonna do anything. As long as you are working that jar, it needs to be shaken daily, and some type of candle needs to be burned on top of it daily while you say your prayers and your petitions over the candle. This goes for any type of work, whether it's love work, money work, jinxes—any type of work that you're doing. If you're working with a jar, these are the steps that you take.

To Sweeten and Draw Money

This work is a work that is done to sweeten and to draw money to you. You need

- a small jar (like a baby food jar)
- some sugar
- a five-dollar bill out of your wallet
- five finger grass
- a magnet
- some Solomon's seal root

You also need a photo of yourself after you have done a cleansing bath, so take the bath first and then take a photo of yourself to use in this work. You need Deuteronomy 30 V 8–10 torn out of the Bible.

Deuteronomy Chapter 30 V 8–10

> 8 And you shall again obey the Lord and observe all his commandments which I command you today. 9 Then the Lord your God will prosper you abundantly in all the work of your hand, in the offspring of your body and in the offspring of your cattle and in the produce of your ground, for the Lord will again rejoice over you for good just as he rejoiced over your father's; 10 if you obey the Lord your God to keep his commandments and his statutes which are written in this book of the law, if you turn to the Lord your God with all your heart and soul.

Place all the ingredients along with the Bible verses into the jar. Blow three breaths into the jar and then close the lid. Shake the jar vigorously so that the ingredients are all mixed up. Then you burn a green tea light candle on top of the jar three times a day while shaking the jar vigorously before you light the candle and pray in your prayer and your petition. The reason you shake the jar is because, if you just leave the ingredients sitting there, once all the prayers and stuff are gone in the jar, then that jar is gonna be useless. You have to keep working the jar, which means you have to keep shaking it and you have to keep a fire going on top of it.

To Slow Someone or Something Down

Have you ever heard the old saying "slow as molasses"? I was taught that you only work with molasses if you want to slow someone or something down. The only exception to this is when I'm working with Big Mama, because molasses is one of her offerings. This jar can be made for many different causes, like court cases dealing with the law, a troublesome person, bill collectors, the list can just go on and on. The basics of the jar stay the same, the only difference is the ingredients that go into the jar.

Before I get started on this, I wanna say this: I have seen a lot of information being shared in different places. I have seen some things that could really be harmful and could really cause money issues and other different kinds of issues by doing that work. I just wanna put this here; this is my experience. Molasses slows things down to a halt. If you do steady work or any type of money work where molasses is involved, and this is just my opinion, I believe that you will slow down your own money. Yes, molasses is very sweet, but it also runs really slow, and if it runs slow, it works slow. You can take this advice with a grain of salt, but I have done my duty by trying to tell you not to use molasses when you are trying to bring things to you unless you were honoring Big Mama or another spirit that has molasses as a offering.

When you are dealing with someone who is causing you problems, this jar will slow them down and stop them. This works with folks who gossip, liars, and all-around troublemakers.

Tear Isaiah 45 V 2 out of the Bible and place it in the jar.

> I will go before you and will level the mountains; I will break down gates of bronze and cut through bars of iron.

As we see in this verse, God will go before you and destroy what is in your way. Add whatever you have of the offenders to the jar, even if it's just their name. Place alum, red pepper, and dirt dauber's nest in the jar. Pour the molasses over everything and add a little whiskey. Close the jar and follow the instructions given on working a jar.

To Slow Down a Court Case

This work is to slow down a court case. You need to tear out Deuteronomy 9 V 8–24. You need to get some dirt from a four-way stop sign; this means a crossroads that has a stop sign on each corner. Add the dirt to the jar, then add the verse on which you have written your name, and place all this in the jar, then pour molasses over it. The opposing side will have nothing but hell through the whole trial, which will give your side time to win your case.

> 8 Also in Horeb you provoked the Lord to wrath, so that the Lord was angry enough with you to have destroyed you. 9 When I went up into the mountain to receive the tablets of stone, the tablets of the covenant which the Lord made with you, then I stayed on the

mountain forty days and forty nights. I neither ate bread nor drank
water. 10 Then the Lord delivered to me two tablets of stone writ-
ten with the finger of God, and on them were all the words which
the Lord had spoken to you on the mountain from the midst of the
fire in the day of the assembly. 11 And it came to pass, at the end of
forty days and forty nights, that the Lord gave me the two tablets of
stone, the tablets of the covenant.

12 Then the Lord said to me, "Arise, go down quickly from here, for
your people whom you brought out of Egypt have acted corruptly;
they have quickly turned aside from the way which I commanded
them; they have made themselves a molded image." 13 Furthermore
the Lord spoke to me, saying, "I have seen this people, and indeed
they are a stiff-necked people. 14 Let Me alone, that I may destroy
them and blot out their name from under heaven; and I will make
of you a nation mightier and greater than they."

15 So I turned and came down from the mountain, and the moun-
tain burned with fire; and the two tablets of the covenant were in
my two hands. 16 And I looked, and behold, you had sinned against
the Lord your God—had made for yourselves a molded calf! You
had turned aside quickly from the way which the Lord had com-
manded you. 17 Then I took the two tablets and threw them out
of my two hands and broke them before your eyes. 18 And I fell[e]
down before the Lord, as at the first, forty days and forty nights; I
neither ate bread nor drank water, because of all your sin which you
committed in doing wickedly in the sight of the Lord, to provoke
Him to anger. 19 For I was afraid of the anger and hot displeasure
with which the Lord was angry with you, to destroy you. But the
Lord listened to me at that time also. 20 And the Lord was very
angry with Aaron and would have destroyed him; so I prayed for

Aaron also at the same time. 21 Then I took your sin, the calf which you had made, and burned it with fire and crushed it and ground it very small, until it was as fine as dust; and I threw its dust into the brook that descended from the mountain.

22 Also at Taberah and Massah and Kibroth Hattaavah you provoked the Lord to wrath. 23 Likewise, when the Lord sent you from Kadesh Barnea, saying, "Go up and possess the land which I have given you," then you rebelled against the commandment of the Lord your God, and you did not believe Him nor obey His voice. 24 You have been rebellious against the Lord from the day that I knew you.

L

Lamps

Lamps will be discussed in section "O" under Oil Lamps. See page 156.

Lemons

Lemons are one of those tools that can be worked for cleansing work, but they can also be worked for works like Shut Your Mouth, separation, and souring work, just to name a few. I know a lot of folks don't like to do what I call "hard works," but sometimes and in some situations, you have to. In the past, I have done works for parents whose children are having a hard time at school. It's not from the other children, it's from the school staff. Most of the time these parents have done the best they can do. They have tried to work with the school to no avail. When they are at the end of their rope, they come to me. It seems there always has to be that one teacher or one principal that has to act like a total ass with some children.

If you find yourself and your child in this type of situation, then this work will help you, and it is an easy remedy. You need

a large lemon
dried red pepper
four needles
a photo of the target

Cut the lemon in half. Take a paring knife and bore holes in each piece of the lemon. Fill the holes with the dried red pepper. Make two copies of the target's photograph. Place them in the lemon where they will be back-to-back. The reason that you are putting those photographs of the target back-to-back is because there's no way that they turn that can get them out of this work. Put the two halves of the lemon together and pin them shut with your needles. Then you place the lemon in a cross setup and pray your petitions over it.

Once the candles burn out, bury the lemon in the west. This will remove the target away from the child. This is a simple, easy work that's powerful. This work can also be done if you have a bully who is bullying your child.

Limes

Limes, like lemons, can be worked with to either sour someone or to remove a cross condition, because the bitterness either cuts or sours. Here is an easy cleansing bath working with a lime. Use this if you find yourself in a situation where nothing is going right, you've had readings done, and nobody's working on you, but you feel like you are stagnated and nothing is moving. This is also good for your skin.

You need to take a white stick candle and brush yourself off with it from head to toe. When you are ready for your bath, you light the candle. Cut a lime in half and petition the Holy Trinity to remove whatever issues you are having. Get in the shower and have your candle burning in a safe place in the bathroom. Clean yourself off with each half of that lime, starting from the top of your head to the bottom of your feet, while you are praying that whatever is there to be gone.

Once you've cleaned yourself off with both halves of the lime, squeeze the lime juice on the top of your head where your crown is. With your hands, vigorously brush down your body, claiming that whatever was there is gone. Make sure that you clean your hands and the bottoms of your feet with both of those limes. Our feet and our hands pick up stuff all during our day; you don't know what's been tricked and what hasn't been tricked. Once you finish your bath, get out and dry off. Leave your candle burning in a safe place. Put the limes in a brown paper bag and throw them away the next day in either a park under a tree or in a crossroads.

Medicine Bottles

When I was coming up as a young worker, medicine bottles were a big thing. When I was a young child, they used to put the medicine in little white envelopes and the prescription was written on the envelopes; then the medicine bottle came out. So the idea of working with medicine bottles is that Conjure is medicine; it does what medicine does and it cures what ails you.

Medicine bottles have been worked for many, many, many years. A lot of new folks don't know about them but back when I was a young worker they were very popular. I work with a lot of medicine bottles and a lot of jars because they contain the works and the more you work them, the stronger the work becomes. I'm going to share a few works where you can work a medicine bottle. This can be any kind of

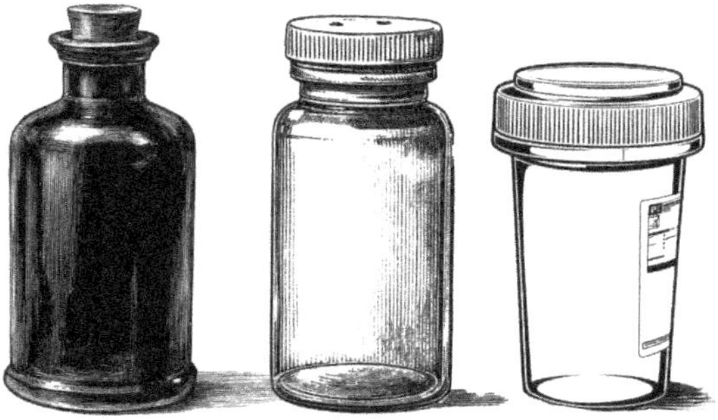

medicine bottle. It can even be a bottle from the pharmacy that the doctor wrote the prescription out for, as long as it has held medicine.

Return to Me

The first work is going to be a Return to Me work. This work is done to draw someone back into your life. Take a photo of your target and wrap the scripture below over the target. Place the photo in a medicine bottle along with a strong magnet. Now I know some folks like to work with lodestones, and I do too in some instances, but in this instance a magnet has a stronger pull, so it is better for this type of work. To the medicine bottle add lovage root, rosemary, lavender, Jezebel root, and Master of the Woods, along with some powdered sugar. Pray your petition into the bottle and close the lid tightly. Shake the bottle while praying your petition. Repeat this daily while burning a tea light on top of the bottle. Keep working the bottle until your target has returned.

Song of Solomon 6 V 1–13

1 Where has your beloved gone,
O fairest among women?
Where has your beloved turned aside,
That we may seek him with you?

2 My beloved has gone to his garden,
To the beds of spices,
To feed his flock in the gardens,
And to gather lilies.

3 I am my beloved's,
And my beloved is mine.
He feeds his flock among the lilies.

4 O my love, you are as beautiful as Tirzah,
Lovely as Jerusalem,
Awesome as an army with banners!

5 Turn your eyes away from me,
For they have overcome me.
Your hair is like a flock of goats
Going down from Gilead.

6 Your teeth are like a flock of sheep
Which have come up from the washing;
Every one bears twins,
And none is barren among them.

7 Like a piece of pomegranate
Are your temples behind your veil.

8 There are sixty queens
And eighty concubines,
And virgins without number.

9 My dove, my perfect one,
Is the only one,
The only one of her mother,
The favorite of the one who bore her.
The daughters saw her
And called her blessed,

The queens and the concubines,
And they praised her.

10 Who is she who looks forth as the morning,
Fair as the moon,
Clear as the sun,
Awesome as an army with banners?

11 I went down to the garden of nuts
To see the verdure of the valley,
To see whether the vine had budded
And the pomegranates had bloomed.

12 Before I was even aware,
My soul had made me
As the chariots of my noble people.

13 Return, return, O Shulamite;
Return, return, that we may look upon you!

Road Opener Medicine Bottle

To make a Road Opener medicine bottle, you need dirt from the four corners of a crossroads and a white hanky. Burn a white tea light candle on the dirt in front of Saint Peter for five days while asking him to open all your roads and to bring you success in everything that you do. The reason you pray for five days is because five is the number of the crossroads and Saint Peter is a road opener.

Once the five days are up, add your dirt to the medicine bottle. To this bottle, you're also going to add a lodestone, a piece of pyrite, your personal concerns, frankincense for protection, a quarter, a dime, a nickel, and a penny. To this, add a little whiskey, some sugar, and some powdered cinnamon. Take a cigar and blow three puffs of smoke into the medicine bottle. Close the lid quickly so the smoke is trapped inside of the bottle. Shake the bottle well while saying your prayer and your petition that your roads be open and that Saint Peter draw in all the goodness to your life that you are looking for and that you need.

You will also need three tea lights a day to burn on top of your medicine bottle. You shake the medicine bottle daily. Say your prayer and your petitions as you are shaking the bottle, then you pray over your tea light, calling, "Saint Peter, didn't you like the tea light?" As the tea light burns, you need to come and say your prayer and petition over the work at least three times while the tea light is burning, if at all possible. The more you work the medicine bottle, the better it is going to work for you.

STFU Medicine Bottle

I wanted to do one more medicine bottle. Folks gossips so bad nowadays, and they seem to have their nose in everybody's business. They feel like they're entitled to know everybody's business. They don't realize, or they just don't care, the damage that their gossip can do to other folks' lives. They feel like it's their business to sweep around other folks' door stoops when the one they're on is overloaded with trash. It's not just the person that does the gossiping, it's also the person that they are toting the tale to, because without them the gossip would die where it started at. So if you have someone in your life that just cannot keep your business out of their mouth, then this medicine bottle is for you. I call it the STFU medicine bottle. The idea behind this bottle is that every single time your name is in the target's mouth, their mouth will burn. Not only that, but the cream of tartar is going to sour their mouth.

They must love this type of stuff because they can't stop sticking their nose in other peoples' business. You need a photo of the target, or simply their name or signature. You are going to take a black permanent marker and write Proverbs 18 V 6–7 across their photograph. You are going to take a lemon or a lime—remember, I said lemons and limes can sour or they can cleanse; well, in this instance we're gonna sour that mouth. Squeeze half of the lemon or lime across the base of the photo. Put some cream of tartar over the photo and then cover that with some hot sauce, the hottest one you can find.

Fold that up and place it inside of the medicine bottle. Then to that bottle, add some hot red pepper, some more cream of tartar, the other half of the lime or lemon, and more hot sauce. Blow three puffs of smoke from a cigar into the medicine bottle and quickly close the lid so the smoke is trapped inside.

Vigorously shake the medicine bottle while you are praying Proverbs 18 verses 6–7 and calling the target's name out after each verse. Burn a tea light candle on the medicine bottle three times a day. Shake the bottle three times a day while praying the Bible verse and calling out the target's name.

Proverbs 18 V 6–7

6 The lips of fools bring them strife, and their mouths invite a beating.

7 The mouths of fools are their undoing, and their lips are a snare to their very lives.

N

Napkins

Dinner napkins can be worked with to draw prosperity into the home. The kitchen is considered by most folks as the heart of the home. This is where most folks gather for dinner. When I was growing up, the kitchen was the place where we all gathered, whether it was for a holiday or we were just visiting my parents. So for me the kitchen is definitely the heart of the home. That is why dinner napkins are so powerful when you are trying to draw in prosperity into the home. You need

- a napkin that was used by the head of the house who makes the most money in the house
- a five-dollar bill out of their pocket
- a pinch of lovage root
- some orange peel
- a pinch of Master of the Woods

Spread the napkin out flat on the kitchen table. Place the five-dollar bill with the face outward, and add the herbs on top of the money along with a tablespoon of sugar. Tie the napkin into a bundle, breathe three breaths on the bundle, and say your petition. Everybody's petition is gonna be different because we all have different needs, so say the petition that goes with whatever you need. Go out the side or back door to the front door of your home. Open the door and throw the bundle into the house—take your foot and gently push that bundle all the way into your kitchen. Once you have it in your kitchen, pick it up and put it on top of the refrigerator.

Once a month feed the bundle either holy oil or money-drawing oil. The bundle should continue to work as long as you feed it. Once a month, say your prayers and petition over the bundle again, as your need may have changed.

Oil Lamps

I have written about oi lamps in my earlier books (e.g., see *Old Style Conjure*) but I am going to reshare the works here because they have been successful for me in the past and they are some of my favorite works. Now, if you've seen some of these works before, you have to understand that not everybody has bought my books and knows about the work that I do with oil lamps. The oil lamp is like a container work with a steady flame burning in the work. This makes them a very powerful tool to use in your work, period. They are very good for long-term work, such as Crown of Success, personal power, court-case work, healing work, enemy work, peaceful-home work, and prosperity work, just to name a few.

As the old workers are dying off, this information is being lost. I think when folks think of oil lamps, they link them to the smell of kerosene, but in this day and age they have a liquid oil called liquid candle oil. It doesn't smell and it burns clean. That is what I use to burn in all my oil lamps. These lamps are safe as long as they don't get knocked over. Just like with any other kind of fire, you have to be careful with them, but they won't bust like a glass candle can. The most they will do is smoke up the top of the lamp if you have the wick too high. It's important to remember that if you buy a used oil lamp, you cleanse it well because you don't know who had the lamp before or what they had going on in their life.

I have found one of the best ways to cleanse something that I've gotten from somewhere else to make sure that I don't pick anything up off of it. It's to cleanse the item just like I would a person if I were doing a spiritual cleansing on them. I cleanse the item off with the egg, just like I would a person, bust the egg, and put it in the water. Then I rinse the item off, if it's possible, with cool, running water, then dress it with either Florida Water or some type of spiritual water that I've made myself. Then I'll let the item air dry before I even try to work with it. I have found that this is an easy way to cleanse lamps that have either been given to me or belonged to someone else.

Oil lamps are an easy way to keep your work going, to keep the flame at a steady flame, and they are easier to load than candles because if you overload a candle then you're either gonna have a fire, or the candle is not gonna burn correctly, or it just won't burn at all. By working with the oil lamp, everything is contained inside the base of that lamp. I'm going to share some oil-lamp recipes that I work with and that I have had good success with.

Remember that after each working with your lamp, when you are finished, you need to recleanse the lamp, so it will be ready for the next time you need to do a working. You don't ever wanna work with something that has not been cleansed, even if you are the one doing the work. You have to clear away the old to bring in the new.

Healing Lamp

I'm speaking to you now as a healer, not a Conjure worker. Healing was the first spiritual work that I ever learned how to do. I was seventeen years old and my son's *madrina's* daddy taught me how to cleanse with eggs, herbs, and candles, because my son was so sick when he was a baby. If you find yourself ill, the first step is to go to a licensed physician (I am not a licensed physician) and make sure that you get the right medication that you need to help with your healing. That should be the very first step that you take. I know nowadays a lot of folks are into self-help healing rituals, but you should always get checked out with a licensed doctor first before you start any type of self-healing rituals.

When you decide that you want to do a healing lamp for yourself or someone else, don't use hot herbs and roots. This could make you or the person you're doing a healing lamp for start running a fever, or it could increase any pain that you or they may be in. Lavender should always be added to a healing lamp because it is so soothing.

Tear Luke 13 V 10–13 out of the Bible.

> 10 On a Sabbath Jesus was teaching in one of the synagogues, 11 and a woman was there who had been crippled by a spirit for eighteen years. She was bent over and could not straighten up at all. 12 When Jesus saw her, he called her forward and said to her, "Woman, you are set free from your infirmity." 13 Then he put his hands on her, and immediately she straightened up and praised God.

Write the name of the person to be healed on the verse and pin it to the bottom of the wick. Add a photo of the person and some hair from the crown of their head, if you can get some. To these ingredients add lavender, allheal, Life Everlasting, angelica root, lemongrass, and three pieces of devil's shoestring that are bound together with a red string to hobble the illness. Pray your prayer into the lamp, then fill the lamp with oil. Set the wick on a low flame. You can set up a small healing altar with photos of the person when they were healthy and felt well. You can add photos and items that remind you of being fit and healthy to the altar. Put an open Bible on the altar, along with some flowers and a cool glass of water. Go to the altar at least three times a day and say your prayer for healing of this person. When you say your prayers, you should say your personal prayers for the healing of the target and you should also pray Luke 13 V 10–13 over the lamp daily as it burns. Keep the lamp going as long as the person needs the help.

Prosperity Lamp

Times are hard and money is tight for everyone right now. I have always kept a prosperity lamp of some type going in my home. For this lamp, take Psalm 23 out of the Bible and pin it to the bottom of the wick. Instead of placing a photo of yourself into the lamp, take a picture of your home and add it to the lamp, or add a photo of your business if you own one. Add hair from the crown of your head. Scrape the bottom of your feet and add the scrapings to the lamp so you will always walk in prosperity.

Now, I know I've said this before, but I think it needs repeating: Before you do any type of prosperity work, you need to do at least one day of spiritual cleansing. You want to make sure that you are spiritually cleansed so you don't drag anything that may be on you into your positive work.

To the lamp add a five dollar bill out of your wallet, a magnet because you want a strong pull, a piece of pyrite, Master of the Woods, bayberry root, a piece of lightning-struck wood if you can get it, five finger grass because the old folks say five finger grass does what five fingers on the hands can do, cinnamon, and frankincense. Once you have the lamp set up, you need to say your prayers and your petitions over this lamp. Now, I didn't dedicate the lamp to any spirit but, for me, I go to Saint Peter with this type of work. Once you get the lamp turned on, make sure that the flame is low so it will burn hot and steady.

Pray Ephesians 1 V 12–21 over your lamp daily. The best way to do this is in three. Three is a very powerful number; it represents the Holy Trinity. Seven is also a very powerful number. It means a job is done, and it's in the Bible many times, like the number three. I know it may seem like a lot, but you have to remember that nothing is free in this life and everything that you get, you have to work for it in one way or another. If you want success with this lamp, you have to do the work. You cannot just let the lamp burn on its own and expect prosperity to fall in your lap. Try to go to the lamp three times a day and say the prayer below along with your petition. Work the lamp for seven days. Keep track of your prosperity and see what a difference the lamp is making in your life. Repetition is power. Anything that you repeat over and over and over becomes a part of you, so do the work and let prosperity flow.

Ephesians 1 V 12–21

12 in order that we, who were the first to put our hope in Christ,
might be for the praise of his glory. 13 And you also were included
in Christ when you heard the message of truth, the gospel of your
salvation. When you believed, you were marked in him with a
seal, the promised Holy Spirit, 14 who is a deposit guaranteeing
our inheritance until the redemption of those who are God's pos-
session—to the praise of his glory. 15 For this reason, ever since I
heard about your faith in the Lord Jesus and your love for all God's
people, 16 I have not stopped giving thanks for you, remembering

you in my prayers. 17 I keep asking that the God of our Lord Jesus Christ, the glorious Father, may give you the Spirit of wisdom and revelation, so that you may know him better. 18 I pray that the eyes of your heart may be enlightened in order that you may know the hope to which he has called you, the riches of his glorious inheritance in his holy people, 19 and his incomparably great power for us who believe. That power is the same as the mighty strength 20 he exerted when he raised Christ from the dead and seated him at his right hand in the heavenly realms, 21 far above all rule and authority, power and dominion, and every name that is invoked, not only in the present age but also in the one to come.

To Destroy an Enemy

Before I give the instructions for this lamp, I want to say this. Before I put up my website in 2006, I had never been thrown at by another worker, and I have trained with some of the best. That thought never crossed my mind. Sure, it happens sometimes when two workers service a small area, but the damn internet goes on and on for infinity. It's a disgrace to the profession. There are more than enough folks out there that need help to supply all the workers who advertise on the internet. There is no need for all this underhandedness that goes on. You should never throw at another worker without a good reason just because you are jealous and too lazy to get your own clients by doing the work to draw them. A seasoned worker would know better than to do something like that. It just shows what a newbie you really are and that you have no experience dealing with other workers in your area.

I keep a lamp just for this reason going at all times on my altar for Big Mama. When this first happened to me, I tried to just let it run its course and move on, but I got sick of it real quick. Now they can throw at me if they want to, but they will get the hoodoo and the what for thrown right back in their faces, plus some. This also shows me and lets me know that these type of folks are either self-taught or learned out of books or off the internet, because one of the first things that young workers are taught is that justification is the foundation of this work. Doing divination and having discernment is important, because you have to know if you are justified in the work that you want to do against someone. Without justification, then you are taking a chance of getting hit with your own work should you go after someone and the work is unjustified. Always make sure that spirit and the spirits that walk with you give you permission to go after another person, and the way you do this is through divination and discernment.

If you are going through this, then this is the type of lamp that should be able to help you even out the playground! As the old folks say, "God don't like ugly." I have no mercy left for these kinds of workers. They have burnt me out of any type of sympathy I might have had within the first two years I was online.

This is a serious lamp and it is not one to play around with, so I'm gonna repeat what I said earlier: Before you do any type of spiritual work, you should do divination first. One, to see if the work is really needed, and two, to see if it's okay to do the work against the target. Like some of my elders said, just because you know how to do something doesn't mean you have to do it, and every action causes a reaction. If you go against someone and they're innocent, you're taking a chance of getting hit with your own work.

For this work you need to tear Exodus 15 V 3–13 out of the Bible and pin it to the bottom of the wick of your lamp. You can use either a straight pin or a safety pin. Like I said, this is a very serious lamp, and Exodus 15 V 3–13 is not something to play around with, as you can see below. The best way to work this lamp is to call for the destruction of all your enemies. Don't call out folks' names; you could have the wrong person. It is better to call for the destruction of all your enemies, known and unknown, rather than someone that you think might be doing something to you. This way you cover all your bases. You have a safety net, so if the wrong person gets hit, that's not up to you, that's up to spirit, and if reversal work is done you will not get hit with your own work because once this work is done, it is out of your hands. It's up to spirit how far spirit goes. Remember this lamp is calling for justice, so the work needs to be justified!

The ingredients for this lamp are

alum
bitter weed
red pepper
a pinch of gun powder
a pinch of sulfur
thorns from a bush
a small blade
Master of the Woods
dirt dauber's nest
calamus root
licorice root
lightning-struck wood
asafetida powder

Once you have all the ingredients loaded into the lamp, you say your personal prayer and petition that this is what you want to happen, and then you pray Exodus 15 V 3–13 three times over the lamp, and you ask God for justice. You need to do this three times a day for twenty-one days.

I just want to stress this one more time because this is such a serious work: If you add someone's name to this lamp and you are wrong about them, if they do a reversal work or if they pray for justice against anybody who is working on them, you will get hit with your own work. It doesn't matter how mad you are at someone; unless you see them doing the work on you, you could be wrong, so just let God be the judge and let him or her handle the situation. You just simply do the work and let them do the rest.

Exodus 15 V 3–13

3 The Lord is a warrior;
the Lord is his name.

4 Pharaoh's chariots and his army
he has hurled into the sea.
The best of Pharaoh's officers
are drowned in the Red Sea.

5 The deep waters have covered them;
they sank to the depths like a stone.

6 Your right hand, Lord,
was majestic in power.
Your right hand, Lord,
shattered the enemy.

7 In the greatness of your majesty
you threw down those who opposed you.
You unleashed your burning anger;
it consumed them like stubble.

8 By the blast of your nostrils
the waters piled up.
The surging waters stood up like a wall;
the deep waters congealed in the heart of the sea.

9 The enemy boasted,
"I will pursue, I will overtake them.
I will divide the spoils;
I will gorge myself on them.
I will draw my sword
and my hand will destroy them."

10 But you blew with your breath,
and the sea covered them.
They sank like lead
in the mighty waters.

11 Who among the gods
is like you, Lord?
Who is like you—
majestic in holiness,
awesome in glory,
working wonders?

12 You stretch out your right hand,
and the earth swallows your enemies.

13 In your unfailing love you will lead
the people you have redeemed.
In your strength you will guide them
to your holy dwelling.

Self-Love Lamp

In this day and time, there is so much going on in this world, and there is so much body shaming on social media. This lamp is meant to help build up a person's self-confidence and to help them love the way they look and to make them feel better about themselves. Our self-esteem can either make us or break us, and depression is a real thing. I think nowadays folks care more about what other folks think about them than what they think of themselves. You can't let someone else dim your light because of what they may think about you. Nobody cares what somebody else thinks about you; you have to care what you think about you. Once we get into that place, it's hard to shake it off sometimes.

I feel like nowadays folks are more open about their lives, about their weaknesses, and then you have others who target those weaknesses because they themselves have low self-esteem. When someone says something negative to you, you should always ask yourself, "Why? Why are they acting that way toward me?" I promise you it has absolutely nothing to do with you. They are making you a target of their own business, of their own failures, of their own negative thoughts and energies about themselves. It has absolutely nothing to do with you.

I wanted to add this lamp because I have found that it has helped me. Everybody has little things about themselves that they wish were better. Everybody can find something wrong with themselves. The problem with that is words are power, and when we talk negative about ourselves, after a while spirit is gonna start to believe that. I was lucky to be raised by a mama who taught us that we could do anything that we wanted to do. We could be anything that we wanted to be. The only thing that could stop us is us. I know a lot of folks are not raised that way, and I know that some folks were not lucky to have a mama like I had, so if this lamp helps one person love themselves then I have done my job.

To make the lamp, you need

- lovage root
- Queen Elizabeth root
- calamus root
- licorice root
- Master of the Woods (these three ingredients together are very powerful; they make you feel like you are in control)
- lavender
- some roses to draw in love
- and anything else that you may be drawn to add

If you're a guy, you can add High John the Conqueror root. Folks say High John is a male root, but there are some women that can work with that root and it works well with them. Do a cleansing bath at least once. Three baths would be preferable, but do at least one. Then take a photo of yourself and pin it to the bottom of the wick of the lamp.

It takes ninety days to change a thought, did you know that? I used to smoke four packs of cigarettes a day, sometimes five if I was stressed out. I literally conjured myself to stop smoking. Every time I would light a cigarette, I would say, "I don't smoke anymore and I don't care if others do," because I never wanted to be one of those ex-smokers that tried to tell other folks that they couldn't smoke. I haven't had a cigarette in about eighteen years. Our minds are powerful, and the mind believes what our eyes see and the words we say to ourselves.

Words are one of the most powerful tools in the world. They are so strong that even a liar can make someone believe that their words are true, even though that person knows better. It's a known fact. So if I were to hold power, and if we can change a thought in ninety days, we can build our self-esteem up so we will be undefeatable and can't be dragged down because we know for a fact that we all that. I don't know everything, but I do know this: When we get dragged down and get out of our character, things in our life start going wrong, and they go wrong because of the way we feel about ourselves. We have to remember that like begets like.

I don't always wake up in a happy mood, but I'll make myself get there. There're times when I slip up and I may think some derogatory thing about myself, but I correct it and that is how you change the way you think about yourself. You do it one step at a time, one prayer at a time, one self-love lamp at a time. Repetition brings power, repetition brings change, and the more you tell spirit something, the more spirit is going to believe what you say, so why not say only positive things about yourself, even if at the time you don't feel positive? Keep track of it and you will notice the change within yourself. Start out gradually, and then before you know it you're so full of yourself you can't even stay in your own self, you think so highly of yourself. That's where you should be.

So I wrote a little prayer down below that you should say at least three times a day over your lamp. Even if you don't feel that it pertains to you, it does. Trust me. You have a right to think very highly of yourself, that's all right. We should think highly of ourselves. We should have a good ego when it comes to our self, just not an ego that takes over because then that's an unbalance. Keep the lamp going for yourself, keep the magic working, build yourself up, and become the person that you wanna be.

I am Love
I am Powerful
I Love Myself
I am the Master of my Life
Love Flows to Me
I am Successful
I am Beautiful
I Love Me!

Attraction Lamp

I do a lot of attraction work for folks, both men and women, where they are trying to draw a new partner into their life. Rather than work on an old partner who has left them, they wanna start fresh. Attraction work to draw a new mate is powerful work, and in this day and time it seems to be needed. I wanna share a tried-and-true attraction lamp that is built to draw in that special person that you are looking for. This lamp is not a one-size-fits-all, because we all are looking for something different within our mate. We don't all need the same type of person or the same type of love; some folks are more needy than others and that's okay. We each have things about us that no one else has, so there is no way one type of attraction lamp or one type of attraction prayer can fit everybody.

When we decide that we want to draw someone new into our life, we need to be very specific about the type of person we are trying to draw into our life. You need to sit down and make a list of all the things that you want in a mate. Don't use phrases like *love me to death, they see only me, they want to be with me only*. These types of statements are going to draw in the wrong type of person. They could literally love you to death. After all, you are working magic here. Magic brings forth change. Spirit brings us what we ask for; spirit cannot tell us what to pray for, so if you're praying the wrong petition, spirit is not going to correct you on that petition.

When you are making out this list of what you want in a mate, be reasonable. Think of the things that you want in your life in a relationship. Peace and happiness should be at the top of the list; having a good job that they love and that they make good money at should be right underneath that.

Before you say "Money don't buy happiness"—that's true, it doesn't—but a broke man or a broke woman is not happy if they are having to struggle just to have food on the table. So no, money cannot buy happiness, but you need money in order to be happy and to live the life that you want to live. You need to be reasonable when you are making this list of attributes that you want this new mate to have. Make sure that you think about the words that you write down in this petition that you are writing for this new love, because words hold power and like begets like. Just be mindful of those things when you sit down and you think about attracting someone into your life. That you're compatible should be one of the main things on that list, and that you can get along with someone who will understand you and who you will understand.

Many marriages have been broken up because of noncommunication. Communication is one of the keys to a happy relationship. I'm sure you get the idea of what I'm talking about. Just make sure that you're reasonable, that you use your common sense, and that you touch on all the bases in all the areas of your life that will make you happy.

For this attraction lamp, you need

- a strong magnet that pulls
- orange peel because it draws
- lavender because it soothes
- Jezebel root if you're a woman where you can be in charge (or High John root if you are male)
- basil for a happy life and protection of your relationship
- red clover to draw in a new love and to promote a strong relationship
- deer's tongue so you can speak in elegance
- Solomon's seal root so you will always have wisdom
- calamus root so you will always be in charge
- lovage root because it not only promotes self-love but also promotes love in general

To fix the lamp, you need to pin your petition, which is what you want in a relationship, to the bottom of the wick. That way, as the wick heats up, the petition heats up. Then you pray over and blow three breaths over each one of the ingredients, and then you add them to the lamp. Once you have the lamp put together, then you need to light it. When you first light this lamp, the flame needs to be a good-sized flame, but make sure that it does not smoke. If it starts to smoke, you have the wick too high.

You need to say your prayer and your petition over the lamp. Your petition should be straight to the point about the qualities that you want in a mate. The fewer words, the better, because sometimes when we overwrite a petition, it not only confuses us, but it also confuses spirit, so in this instance more is not better.

The petition should be able to flow when you are praying it. This work should be done three times a day, and you keep the work going until you have achieved what you are asking for. This is not the type of work that I can give you the exact combination to, because along with the ingredients, you have to add your own heartfelt petition, and you are the only one that can do that. I can't do that for you. The more you work the lamp, the stronger it will become. And I feel like I need to say this: Our time is not spirit's time, so if you feel like the lamp is not working fast enough, you need to remember that God is never late. The spirits run by their own clocks; our time ain't their time. You cannot get discouraged and you cannot stop the work. You have to keep pushing.

Sometimes when things don't work fast enough, it could be because we're missing something, or there is something that we need to fix within our own self. As I have said over and over, like begets like. If you have low self-esteem, that's the kind of person you're gonna draw into your life. If you have negative thoughts about yourself, that's the kind of person you're gonna draw into your life. So make sure that your self is together so you can draw the person that you want and need in your life to make you happy.

Just Judge Lamp

Things happen sometimes that are out of our control, and it could involve the court system. I do a lot of justice work for my clients. There are a lot of Just Judge prayers out there, but I wrote my own because when you say a prayer and a petition, it needs to flow. Just Judge works for anything that you are being unjustly accused of. Whether it be the court system or the court of your peers, if you are being unjustly accused, then you can petition the Just Judge to set it right. Oil lamps are traditionally what was worked with because that's what they had at home. They had kerosene right at hand, the lamps were there, and since this work is all about tricks, I'm pretty sure that they burned those lamps sometimes right in front of the target.

If you find yourself in need of a Just Judge lamp, these are the ingredients that you could work with. You need to take Proverbs 18 V 5 out of the Bible. Pin the verse to the wick of the lamp. Use a safety pin to pin the verse. Then, to the lamp, you need to add some dirt from a courthouse, deer's tongue, barberry root, basil, and devil's bit to hobble the devil. You need to add either paperwork ash that pertains to the court case or personal items of the target to the lamp. Once you have all the ingredients in the lamp, you need to pray Proverbs 18 V 5 three times over the lamp. You should also pray three Our Fathers, three Hail Marys, and three Apostles' Creeds. Once you have the prayers done, go ahead and pour your lamp oil into the lamp. Close the lid on the lamp and light the wick. Adjust the wick so the flame burns a little high at first, but not high enough to smoke.

Proverbs 18 V 5

It is not good to be partial to the wicked or to deprive the righteous of justice.

Now you can either say the prayer that I've written, which I've had good results with, or you can find the Just Judge prayer online, or you can write your own. You need to say the prayer over the lamp at least three times a day. After each verse you say your petition. You keep the lamp going until the case is solved and justice has been served.

Just Judge Prayer

I call on the most High Judge, he who has the last word,

The one who sits at the right hand of God,

The one born of the Holy Mother Mary,

The one who holds the scales of Justice,

You, Father, hold the power to give me Justice,

I ask Father that those who have harmed me be brought to justice,

May they be brought to their knees and feel the power of your justice,

I come before you, Father, and ask that Justice be served!

In the Holy name of God the Father, God the Son, and
God the Holy Spirit.
Amen.

Saint Martha the Dominator Lamp

I have worked with Saint Martha the Dominator for many, many, many years. A lot of folks only see her as a dominator of men, but she is so much more. She can be petitioned for protection, for healing, for justice, and, yes, for dominance, but she is not just a dominator. She works mostly with women, but she will work with some men. I've known men that she works with well for them. I don't know what it is about them that she decides to help them, but most men stay clear of her. My grandsons are drawn to her, so maybe it's just something about the spirit of the male that she decides to help. I don't know. What I do know is that she is very powerful and that when you call on her she comes and she works fast. For about twenty years she sat on a shelf in my kitchen. I tried moving her many times and couldn't. She stayed there until one day it just came in my mind to move her, so I moved her by the door in my living room, and that's where she's been.

She is very good at defense work when you need defending against an enemy. She will also help you if you find yourself in a situation where you don't know which way to turn. She will guide you and help you find your way out of the situation. Of course, anything dealing with a man, she is quick to get on it. So if you find yourself in the need of Saint Martha the Dominator's help, you can do this lamp for her.

For the lamp you need

calamus root
licorice root
barberry root
Master of the Woods
master root

If you notice, all those roots are roots that can dominate a target. Barberry root is worked with to bar your enemies. I added the prayer that I wrote for Saint Martha below. You can work with the prayer that I wrote or you can get one of the prayers that are online and work with that. I'm gonna say this before we go further though: If you petition Saint Martha, you can't just do whatever you want and you can't just petition her to go after someone because they made you mad. You shouldn't petition any saint or spirit when you're mad anyway.

Once you have the lamp going, you need to say three Our Fathers, three Hail Marys, and three Apostles' Creed. Then you say the prayer and your petition over the lamp to Saint Martha. Make sure to give her an offering. It could be coffee, flowers, whatever you feel drawn to give her, but give her something because she works hard.

Once the job is over you can either leave the lamp there and burn it in her honor, or you could put it away until it is needed again.

Saint Martha the Dominator Prayer

Holy Mother St Martha I come to you in desperate need,

Blessed Mother I ask that you come to my aid,

I ask Holy Mother you who walks with me to
intercede on my behalf,

Mother, I pray that you will hold my enemy down
like you did the dragon under your feet,

Stop my enemies from harming me blessed Mother,
protect me! Amen

Steady-Work Lamp

There are times when we need a little help finding a job or to get our current job to give us more hours. Times are hard right now and work is slow going for everybody. If you find yourself in a situation where you are having to look for employment or you need your employer to give you more hours, then this lamp may be able to help you. First let's look at the situation. If you already have a job and you just need more hours, the lamp is worked a little differently, because you're already working and not looking for a job. You need a business card, a signature, or a photo of the person that fixes the schedule at your job. You need some lavender so that the job runs smooth, and all the aggravation is cut out of it, some orange peel to pull that person closer to you to favor you, a pinch of sugar, some calamus root, and some basil to draw in blessings. Take one of your check stubs from when you were making your forty-plus hours and pin it to the wick of the lamp. You're going to say your prayer and petition over the lamp, fill it, and light the lamp. You are going to pray Psalm 23 over that lamp daily. When it comes to the verse that says "I shall not want," stress that; that's God's promise to us that we would never be without.

Now if you're looking for a new job, then to your lamp you need to add dirt from the company you want to work at. You could simply drop a damp napkin and pick it up—it's gonna pick up the dust off the floor, or wipe a window sill with it, or just get a rock or a little bit of dirt from outside of their building. You need either a business card, the name or a photo of the person who does the hiring and who you will have the interview with. You add those things to your lamp. You need some lavender so the interview runs smoothly, a magnet to pull the person who does the interview to you, some calamus, some basil, and you need some gravel root along with some Solomon's seal root so you will have the wisdom to know the right things to say in the interview. You also need to place your photo at the bottom of the wick. Just pin it there with a safety pin.

Once the lamp is put together, you are going to say your personal prayer over the lamp. Fill the lamp and light it. Every day you are going to pray Psalm 23 over that lamp and you will also say your own personal prayer. Once you have the job, you can still keep the lamp going for a while to make sure that you're favored at work. This lamp can also be customized to fit your needs. Nothing is written in stone. If you have a different situation, the lamp can be put together to fit that situation. It all depends on why you are doing the work. If you are drawn to put different roots and herbs in the lamp, or work with a different prayer, that's up to you. You can make the lamp fit what you need.

Psalm 23

1 The Lord is my shepherd; I shall not want.

2 He maketh me to lie down in green pastures: he leadeth me beside the still waters.

3 He restoreth my soul: he leadeth me in the paths of righteousness for his name's sake.

4 Yea, though I walk through the valley of the shadow of death, I will fear no evil: for thou art with me; thy rod and thy staff they comfort me.

5 Thou preparest a table before me in the presence of mine enemies: thou anointest my head with oil; my cup runneth over.

6 Surely goodness and mercy shall follow me all the days of my life: and I will dwell in the house of the Lord for ever.

Bonus: How to Make an Oil Lamp

Not everyone has the money to buy an oil lamp, so you cannot let that stop you. You can make your own oil lamp out of a tin can and some cotton for the wick. You can work with whatever size tin can you have. You need to keep the top of the can because that is what is going to hold your wick in place. I'm gonna give you two different ways to set the wick. You will need an ice pick or a nail in order to put a hole in the top, so you will have a place to run the wick. You can work with a store-bought wick or you can roll a wick out of cotton; either way works. Clean the can well. Make a hole in the top of the can lid. Try to get it centered as best as possible. Run the wick through the hole. Make sure that the wick is long enough where you have some hanging down in the can. The lid from the can should sit perfectly around the edges of the can where you cut the lid off to start with. Then you can load your roots and herbs, and place your oil (and you can burn vegetable oil in the can, you don't have to use liquid candle wax oil). These make good lamps and they're inexpensive. They work well, and they really don't smoke if you don't pull too much wick out.

Another way to make a wick is what I call a floating wick. Take a piece of cardboard and cut it into a round circle that will fit inside of the can. Then you wrap the cardboard with tinfoil so the oil or the fire from the wick cannot get to the paper. Make sure that you cover it with at least two pieces of tinfoil. Then you make a hole in the center and you run the wick through the hole. Place your ingredients into the can and then add your oil. Place the wick on top of the oil and light the wick. Eventually it will get saturated with oil. When that happens, you simply have to make another one. These are good for one-and-done jobs where you might not want to reuse the lamp again, but they are also good when you don't have an oil lamp and you don't have any candles. You should have all these things at home already.

Packets

I want to give the basic instructions for making a packet, but first I think I need to be clear on what a packet is. Packets are similar to Conjure bags, mojo bags, and gris gris, only a packet is made from about a four-by-four-inch piece of red flannel that is made into a small packet. You can even make them larger; it depends on what you are making the packet for. Normally packets are something that can be placed in a pocket or in a lady's undergarments. They're not as large as a Conjure bag, but they carry just as much of a punch.

I usually make my packets with three to five herbs because it is a small packet. You gather all your ingredients, you pray over each ingredient, and you lay it on top of the flannel. If you have something that belongs to the target, if it's a photo or if you're just adding their name, burn it to ash, because not only does the fire heat the work up, but it also makes what you're adding smaller.

Once you have the material loaded, you need to fold the packet. I'm gonna give two different ways to fold this packet, because it can be made for many different things. If you are trying to get someone to do something for you, then you're going to fold the packet toward you. Once you get the packet folded, then you're gonna take a needle and a thread, and you are going to stitch it shut. On each stitch, you are going to say your prayer and your petition: what it is that you want the target to do, the reason for making the packet. Once you have the packet made, then you need to feed the packet some whiskey. You just put a few drops on it and set the packet in a candle setup. Since you are trying to draw somebody to you to do something for you, then you are going to set the candles down in a cross setup. The way you do that is top to bottom, and right to left, because you want to send spirit out to draw whatever it is that you're trying to bring in to you.

Now if you are trying to remove something or someone away from you because they are doing something to harm you or something to cause you issues, then you add your ingredients to the packet. This time you're going to fold the packet away from you, and on each stitch you are going to say your prayer and petition that this person, thing, or issue be locked down and/or be removed away from you. When you set the candles down for this work, you're going to set them down top to bottom, left to right. You are crossing over the packet to lock down whatever it is that you are trying to get control of you. Light the candles the same way you set them down. This is basically the way you make a packet.

Lucky Hand Packet

To put this packet together, you need a piece of red flannel, Psalm 93 torn out of the Bible, Master of the Woods, some tobacco, and you need your personal items that you wanna add to the packet. You need Queen Elizabeth root if you're a woman and High John root if you're a man. You can find the instructions on how to make a packet up above. Cut your small piece of fabric, then you're going to place the Psalm and then add each one of your ingredients one at a time after you have prayed over them and blown three breaths over each one of them.

Once you have all the ingredients on the prayer, you fold the prayer into a small packet, set the packet on the red flannel, and then you sew the packet up. On each stitch you will say your prayer and your petition. Once you have the packet, some call on Saint Peter and ask him to fill the packet with his power. Ask him to give you power and luck. Give the packet to Saint Peter for three days, then on the fourth day take the packet and feed it some whiskey. You can either wear the packet or carry it in your pocket, but you need to keep the packet on you at all times.

Protection Doll Head

This next work is loading a doll head that can be worked to fool your enemy. This is not a doll baby, but a doll head, because it takes all the hits that are being thrown at you. Anytime you are crossed up, blocked, or spiritually attacked, your head is the first place to get hit. If someone is dominating you with work, they'll try to get in your head to confuse you and make you do whatever it is that they want you to do. Confusion is the number one sign you are being conjured, because to hide their work some workers will confuse you so you won't realize that you are even under attack. This stands to reason, because if you know you are being hit, then you'll cleanse yourself and reverse whatever is being done so it can go back to the sender.

The doll head works by confusing your enemies and making them think it's you. It confuses the spirits being called on to dominate or bring you trouble. It is also good because the doll head protects you and removes all kinds of blocks. This type of Conjure doll head is different from what you normally hear about because it uses the link to your spirit to fool your enemies.

When I was young, my grandma used to wear her used drawers at certain times on her head or wrap them around her neck. She swore up and down that if you were being crossed up, your drawers would protect you by removing the work being put on you. In one of Harry Hyatt's books, there's a really old work where you take your worn shirt, turn it inside out, and put it behind your door at the hinges to protect you from having roots thrown on you. This work is something my elders all used to do.

Did you know you can soak your used underwear in coffee and put it on the back of your neck to remove cross conditions? You can also tie a white handkerchief around used coffee grounds and place it between your shoulder blades and the back of your neck to remove cross conditions.

To make the doll head, you first need to take a regular bath before you go to bed. You need to wear an old shirt that you can wear around town during the day, and then go to bed wearing it at night. Wear that old shirt all day the next day until it's time to take your bath again. Run a tub of water, get in the tub with the shirt on, and take your bath. Before you rinse off, take this shirt off over your head and keep it wrong side outwards. Put it in the sink and leave it there to drip dry. Do not wring the shirt out. If you do that, you'll remove all your personal essence from the shirt. Leave the shirt in the sink until it is half dry, then hang it up and let it dry the rest of the way. Once the shirt is dry, take it out and fold it longways in half, then fold it again, going away from you to take off cross conditions and remove hits. This is what is going to make the head of the doll.

In the center of the folded material, place

- your photo
- hair from the crown of your head
- devil's bit
- devil's shoestring
- angelica root
- frankincense
- myrrh
- Jezebel root if you are a woman
- a razor blade to cut your enemies
- dirt dauber's nests to confuse your enemies
- Master of the Woods for power

Fold your shirt around the ingredients going away from you until you can't fold it anymore. Wrap red satin around the head, because now you've got a head. Then you have to stitch it closed. Say your prayer on every stitch you make. You can decorate your head any way you want to, but you need to at least make a face and put a large magnet on top of the head to draw anything that's thrown at you into the head. Once your head is done, give it a drink of whiskey and place a tea light candle on top of the magnet.

You should feed the doll head once a month with whiskey to keep it strong, and continue covering it with protection powder to keep it working for you. When you feed the doll head, light a tea light once again on top of the magnet.

Remember, this doll head represents you. Be very careful with it. Make sure that any enemy cannot get ahold of this head. Take care of the doll head and it will take care of you. As long as you feed it and give it a candle, it should continue to work. It might not catch everything but it's going to be a big help if you put it together right and you take care of it.

Papier-Mâché

I love working with papier-mâché. It is really easy to hide a work with it. Papier-mâché is nothing more than strips of paper that have been dipped in glue and made into a form. When the form is still wet, you can use a knife and cut a small hole in it, then you can load your ingredients into the form and seal it back up. No one will ever know that that is work. All they are going to see is something pretty that you made out of papier-mâché. This is a sneaky way to do domination, controlling assets, Bend Over, and all types of love works. You can leave the works out near the target and they will never know that they are being conjured.

For those who don't know how to make papier-mâché, it is very easy, but nowadays it seems to be a hot item in the craft stores. You can find just about anything made out of papier-mâché. If you want to do this work, then you need an item made out of papier-mâché, a brown paper bag, some paints of your choosing, a sharp blade, and the ingredients that go along with the job you're going to do. The first thing you need to do is to cut a small slit in the back of your papier-mâché art. Then you hold the item up to your mouth and, where you made the slit at, you pray your petition into the hollow opening of the papier-mâché art. Place your art piece in a candle setup working with five tea lights, say your prayers and petition over the piece, then gather up the rest of your ingredients. You will set the tea lights down in the shape of a cross, and the last tea light will be set on top of the art piece you are working on.

Lay out a white handkerchief so you will have somewhere to place your ingredients. Pick up each ingredient and say your prayer and petition over the ingredients. Once you have prayed over all of the ingredients, place the tea light on top of the ingredients. Light the tea light, and let it burn. Once the tea light burns out, load your papier-mâché art with the ingredients that go with the work. Then tear a couple of pieces of brown paper bag so you can seal the slit in your art. To do this, you need some Elmer's glue that you have added water to. This is kind of messy, but it will seal up the slit and no one will ever be the wiser. Dip the paper in the glue wash, lay the paper over the slit, and press the paper down gently. Smooth it out where it won't tear and there will not be any lumps. Layer about three pieces of paper over the slit, then set your art out in the sun to dry. Once it is dry you can decorate it any way you want to. Then you once again place it in a candle setup and pray your prayers and petitions over it. When it is done you just set it out wherever it is that you want to put it and let it do its job. This is a good way to hide your work in plain sight.

Now, there is another way that you can prepare the glue when you are ready to do a work. The ingredients will depend on what job you are doing. In order to make the glue wash for the papier-mâché, you have to add water. When I have a work that I need to do, if I'm gifting a gift to someone, or if I'm making something for my home, and I wanna draw in blessings, I will make a wash with the roots and herbs, strain the wash, and use that wash water to thin out the glue. You just have to be careful to make sure that you don't add too much water, because if the glue is too runny it will not work. Then you can take whatever ingredients that you are going to load the art piece with and place those inside of the papier-mâché piece. By adding the herbal wash to the glue, the piece is basically worked on the inside and the outside. Just another way to do the work.

Large Dried Peppers

The dried red pepper makes a wonderful Conjure tool. Making a packet out of a dried red pepper is easy; you just have to be careful when you cut the slit in the pepper. These peppers are paper thin. I have a work that has been in my Black Hawk bucket for at least ten years, and it is still working. Once a month I take it out and feed it and place the packet in a circle candle setup. I use the circle setup with this packet because a circle is never-ending. Nothing can get in and nothing can get out.

I'm going to give you the instructions to make two different kinds of packets—the Pay Me packet, and the Stay-at-Home packet. First, I want to give you the instructions on how to make the packet.

Try to find the largest red dried pepper you can find at the supermarket. Take a sharp knife or blade. Be very careful and cut a slit about three inches long in the pepper. Gently pull the pepper apart so you have an open end the length of the slit. To keep the slit open while you're working, roll a piece of paper towel up and gently place it in the slit. This will hold the pepper open while you get your ingredients together. This way when you're ready to load the pepper, it won't be so hard to handle. That pepper is hot, so you might wanna wear gloves. Do not remove the seeds from out of the pepper.

You will have to wrap the pepper with red cotton thread because you cannot sew the pepper shut. A needle and thread would tear the pepper apart because it is so thin. Once you get the paper wrapped, you need to make a packet with either red flannel or a white handkerchief. I prefer red flannel, but I have seen elders use both to make the packet. You need your material, some red cotton thread, and a needle.

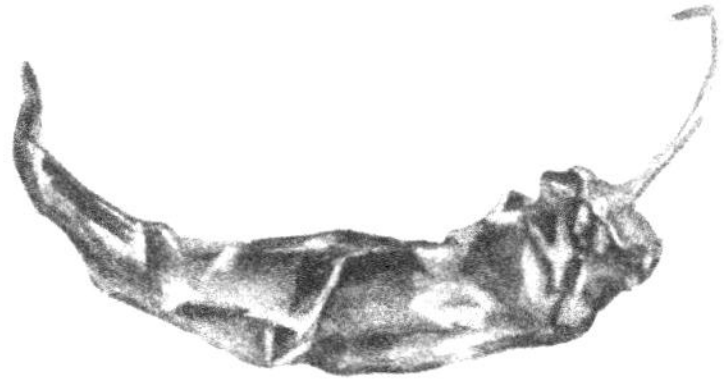

Lay the pepper in the center of the material. Fold the material toward you if you are drawing something. If you are removing something, then fold the material away from you. Once you have the packet made, start at one end and make three knots. On each knot you will say, "In the name of God the Father, God the Son, and God the Holy Spirit." Then you whipstitch all the way around the packet while praying your prayer and petition. Call on the Holy Trinity, your ancestors, and the spirits of the target. Once you have the packet made, you feed the packet with some whiskey and place it in a candle setup. Make sure you go and say your prayers and petition over the work as long as the candles are burning.

Pay Me Packet

Through my clients, I have come to the realization that folks don't pay back money they owe. It seems like this has become a common thing. I have so many clients that have come to me for Pay Me visuals to be burned to try to recoup the money that is owed to them. This Pay Me packet has worked well for me over and over again, so here are the instructions on how to make it if you have a target that owes you money and refuses to pay it back.

In each of these works I'm going to give you, you follow the basic instructions that can be found at the beginning of the Packets section on page 181.

For this packet, you need calamus root, licorice root, dirt dauber's nest, and Master of the Woods. If at all possible, get a coin or a dollar from the target. You can work with either a photo of the target or their name. Burn the photo to ash. Mix it with all the other ingredients. Bring the ingredients up close to your mouth and pray your prayers and petitions over the ingredients. Load your ingredients into the pepper and then follow the instructions above.

Stay-at-Home Pepper Packet

There are times when our spouses or partners just can't seem to stay at home. They are more interested in what is going on in the streets than they are in what is going on in their own families. I'm a firm believer that if you make a commitment, then you should keep that commitment. If you can't, then at least be honest and get to moving around. There is no such thing as having your cake and being able to eat it too. Someone always gets hurt when folks try to do this. Everyone deserves to have an honest and true mate. If your better half doesn't want to be without you and at the same time doesn't want to stay off the streets, then it's time to step in and take over.

If you find yourself in a situation with your partner and nothing has seemed to work, try this pepper packet. I want to make this very clear from the start: This is not some sugary work. You are taking total control over the situation. This does not mean that you have a license to walk all over your mate. That would be no different than what they are doing to you. It does mean that this will help give you a way to stop all the running around and being on the streets. I just want to make that clear that you follow the basic instructions as above. For this work, you need the heel of a dirty, worn sock, calamus root, licorice root, dirt dauber's nest, and Master of the Woods. Before we get into how to put this together, some of you may be wondering why you use the heel out of a dirty sock. First off, that sock has been on the target's feet, and what do our feet do? They walk us wherever we need to go. Also it has picked up his essence. Have you ever heard the old saying that "she has him under her heel"? This is basically what you are doing; you are getting the target under your feet using something that his own feet had been in to make him or her walk the line.

Burn the sock to ash and mix it with all the other ingredients. Hold the ingredients up to your mouth and pray your prayer and petition, then load the ingredients into the dried red pepper. Then you follow the instructions above to put the pepper packet together.

Pincushion

I love pincushions. You are never going to look at them the same way again. Did you know that the pincushion that your auntie or grandma has could have Conjure work going on underneath it? I found a pincushion that belonged to my mother. The top was being held on by a ribbon. When I undid the ribbon and looked underneath it, there were little slips of paper under there that were nailed down when the pins were stuck into the cushion. The writing is so faded I can't tell what it is, but I left them under there. Working with a pincushion, there is no need to stick pins in a doll baby.

You can make your own pincushion. You need a round piece of wood, some cotton (cotton is important because cotton absorbs), some fabric to cover the cushion with, and some ribbon. Glue the

cotton to the thin piece of wood. Make sure you have enough cotton layered so it stands up about two inches above the wood. Take your fabric and pull it over the cotton, then you tie the material on to the cotton puff with a pretty ribbon. You can work with the pincushion in the normal way, but then when you have an issue that needs to be handled, all you have to do is take the cover off the pincushion, place either the target's photo, their name, or your petition inside, place the cover back over the cushion, and stick the pin in. Then, every time you stick a needle in the pincushion, say your prayer and your petition over the target. This is also a tricky work that is right there in plain view, but folks will never know what it is unless you tell them.

You can get the cotton shapes at any hair supply. When you are making your pincushion, you can layer roots and herbs within the folds of the cotton. Of course, you know that if this is going to be a Conjure tool then it has to be worked before you can utilize its power as a working tool. I remember my auntie using a sock that she had tied into a knot as a pincushion. At the time I was too young and didn't realize what she was doing, but I do know that that sock belonged to my uncle who was known to get out of control. Conjurer work is about being tricky. It's about hiding works in plain sight. This pincushion is just another way to hide the work in plain sight and get it next to a target. Even if you don't sew you can make a pincushion for your work and just leave it sitting around until you need it. It is an easy way to nail situations and targets down.

Plants

Working with plants is one of my favorite types of work. Plants are a living, breathing thing, and working with them in magic really makes the work stronger. As long as you keep the plant alive, your work will stay alive. That's the key to success with this kind of work: You have to make sure that your plant lives and thrives. If the plant dies, your work dies.

I love working with lush green plants. To me these dark plants represent prosperity. I prefer to work with either an ivy or a fern for prosperity work. To do this, you need to find a good, healthy plant, a nice pot, and you need some red flannel to make the packet. (The instructions for making the packet can be found on page 181.) You need some money from your pocket, some licorice root, Master of the Woods, bayberry, orange peel, and dirt from the four corners of your property.

Place all your ingredients in a circle setup with tea light candles. As you light each tea light, pray your prayer and your petition for prosperity. Once you have your packet ready, place it in your pot that you will be planting your plant in. Take the plant gently out of the container and hold the roots up close to your mouth. Pray your prayer and petition over the roots. Push your breath forward so it flows over the roots of your plant. Gently put your plant in your pot, then give your plant a cool drink of water. Talk to the plant daily. As long as you nurture and take care of your plant, your prosperity should grow as the plant grows.

Remember, the plant is a living thing and the magic is a living thing. Again, if you let the plant die, the magic dies along with it. So make sure that you take really good care of any plant that you are doing magic with.

Loading a Plaque

Plaques are an easy way to hide your work in plain sight. Back in the day, when I was growing up, folks made statues and things out of chalkware. You can still find the forms for chalkware. If you search online, you can find forms that you can pour that are the images of some of the saints. I have made these chalkware plaques for families and in-house clients, but you have to have a mold. Another good thing about this type of work is that you can use spiritual oils as a nonstick agent in your mold.

All you have to do is pour the chalkware mix into the mold, then you can add your ingredients—the photos, the petitions, whatever it is that you are going to add to the work. While the plaque is drying, set it in a candle setup, then pray your prayer and your petitions over it while it dries. Once it dries, then you can hang it up in your home somewhere and no one will ever know that it's a spiritual item unless you tell them. This is Conjure in plain sight.

As a side note, nowadays they have all these little soap molds and all types of molds that you can buy. Those can also be used for chalkware. You have to make sure that they are heat resistant, because the chalkware mix does get warm. There are a lot of things that you can trick out, working with those molds. Your imagination is the limit; you have to look at everything with the eyes of a worker. If it can be put together, it can be worked.

Railroad spikes are worked with when you want to nail someone down, or they can be worked with for protection. I'm going to give you two different works that can be worked with by placing a fixed packet to the railroad spike. One work will be for protection and the other work will be to nail an enemy down.

Before you can work with the railroad spike, the spike itself needs to be cleansed. You cleanse it by putting it under cool, running water, then you let it air dry. Once it's dry, you need to cover it with rock salt and leave it covered for three days. When the three days are up, you take it out of the rock salt and you brush it off. Do not wash it again. The last step is to bathe it in Florida Water and let it air dry. A lot of folks work with these railroad spikes to nail down their property, and this is the way you get them ready to put them to work. You don't want to take a railroad spike that you just got from somewhere and nail it down on your property, because you don't know what kind of energies that spike has picked up. You should always clean any type of tool that you are working with before you put it to work.

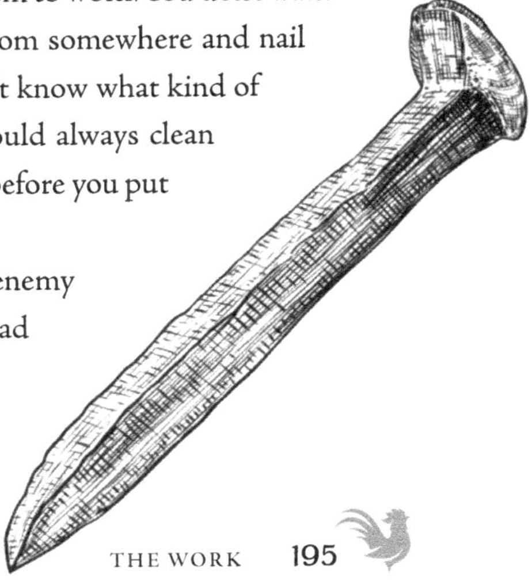

This first work is going to be to nail an enemy down. The first step is to cleanse the railroad spike, per instructions above. Although I have written about how to make a packet, I am going to touch on it again here. To make a packet, you need a piece of material. Red flannel is usually the material that is worked with, although if you can get a piece of dirty clothing from your target, that will work even better. You need to cut about a four-by-four-inch or a six-by-six-inch piece of material; it all depends on the ingredients that you are going to be working with. Bulky ingredients take more cloth in order to make the packet. Once you have your material cut, you need to lay out your ingredients one by one, and you also need to pray over them before you add them to the cloth.

There come times in our lives when folks just don't know how to act. They feel like they can do or act any kind of way that they want to, and that you are supposed to put up with it. Life isn't like that. Nobody has a right to overstep themselves and expect people to just deal with it. If you find yourself in this type of situation, then this railroad spike may be able to help you.

In the Southern culture, you will hear folks say, "Not today, Satan." They are not necessarily talking about the devil; any actions that goes against you and your peace of mind is a devil. This packet is to nail a devil down, which in normal talk means nailing down a person who is overstepping themselves and doing too much. For this packet, you need devil's shoestring, devil's bit, and devil's pod. You will also need calamus, licorice root, Master of the Woods, a photo of the target, and/or their personal concerns if you have them, if not the photo will work fantastic. If you don't have their photo, then you can work with their name only. You need to pray over each ingredient three times.

Anything with the name of the devil in it is worked with to hobble the devil, which means to nail your enemy down. So pray over the devil's shoestring, the devil's bit, and the devil's pod that it is your petition that God hobble the devil in your life, remove them away from you, and tie them up where they can no longer cause you issues. Over the calamus root, the licorice root, and the Master of the Woods, you pray and petition that you become the master over your enemy. You do the same thing over their photo. You place the photo on the cloth and then you add each one of your ingredients after you have prayed over them.

Fold the cloth away from you into a small packet. Wrap it three times around going away from you. Make three knots in the thread and as you make each knot say, "I bind [so and so] in the name of God the Father, I bind [so and so] in the name of God the Son, I bind [so and so] in the name of God the Holy Spirit." Once you get your three knots done, then you can finish wrapping the packet where it will stay closed, and you tie it off with three knots. When you have the packet done, then it is time to bind that packet to the railroad spike.

You repeat the same process. Wrap the thread around the packet and spike three times, then you tie your three knots. Say, "I bind [so and so] in the name of God the Father, in the name of God the Son, and in the name of God the Holy Spirit." Then you continue wrapping the packet to the spike while you are saying your prayers and your petitions. Once you feel like the packet is secure, then you're going to tie off your last three knots, and again say, "I bind [so and so] in the name of God the Father, God the Son, and God the Holy Spirit."

When you have this spike ready, then you need to set it up in a triangle setup. You set the candles down top, left corner, right corner. You are going left to right because you are trying to nail down the target. You light your candles the same way you set them down. You say your prayers and your petition over each candle three times as you light it. When the candles burn out, the spike should be ready.

Just wrap it up in a white handkerchief and put it in a safe place. Once a month, you need to set the spike in a triangle setup and feed the packet some whiskey in order to keep it working. When there is no longer an issue, you can cut the packet off the spike, burn the packet, place the ashes in the west, and cleanse the spike so it can be worked with again.

I said I was only gonna give two works with the railroad spike, but I think I'm gonna give three. The reason is because folks who live in apartment buildings cannot nail their homes down the same way as folks who live in a house or who live on their own property can, and we all need to be able to feel like we are safe in our own homes. So I'm gonna give this short, little work, and then we're gonna move on to the protection work.

If you live in an apartment and it doesn't belong to you, then the land the dirt is from is only temporary. If you move, then that spike would have to be undone. You can work this by having plants in the four corners of your home, your apartment. You work the spikes and bury them in the plants. You would follow the instructions above about how to cleanse the spikes and then you would fix them to your apartment. I know some folks live in their apartments for up to twenty to twenty-five years. So as long as you live in that apartment and you keep those plants alive, those spikes should work just like they would if they were nailed down on the land if you were nailing down your property. The thing is that you have to keep those plants alive. If the plants die, the work dies. If you ever move, you can remove the spikes from the plant, cleanse them, and, if you're moving into another apartment, you simply fix them to that apartment.

Spikes are really good for protection. Anything iron, it's really good for protection, because iron is hot. It's also almost impossible to bend or break. I want to give a protection work working with a spike and a packet. You cleanse your railroad spike just like you would for any other type of work that you would be working with a railroad spike for (the instructions are above). For the packet, you need a red piece of flannel, either a four-by-four-inch, or six-by-six-inch, depending on the size you need the packet to be. You need dirt from the four corners of your house and the four corners of your land. Set the dirt on top of the square piece of red flannel. Remember to pray over the dirt. To the dirt you need to add angelica root, lavender, calamus root, three pieces of devil's shoestring to hobble the devil, and a small blade or a razor blade. Be very careful with the sharp objects. You also need to spiritually cleanse your home and then take a photo of the house. Place the photo on top of the ingredients and fold the fabric into a packet. Using red cotton thread, wrap the packet three times, then you are going to make three knots. On each knot, you are going to say, "This home is protected in the name of God the Father, in the name of God the Son, and in the name of God the Holy Spirit." On the Holy Spirit, make the last knot. Once you have the knots made, then you continue to wrap the packet until you have it wrapped up tightly. Then once again you're going to make three knots, praying your prayers and petitions and calling on the Holy Trinity.

Once you get the railroad spike finished, you need to feed the packet some whiskey and place it in a cross setup. The first candle should be placed at the top, the second one at the bottom, the third one at the left side, and the fourth candle to the right. The reason you are crossing over the railroad spike is because you are nailing down the protection work that is supposed to protect you and your home. You need to do this work for seven days. Seven is the number of things being finished. During the time when the candles are burning, you should go every day, at least three times a day, and say your prayer and your petition. Call on the Trinity until the candles burn out.

When the candles burn out, then it's time to take your protection spike and place it behind the door where folks come in and out of your house. The reason I say that is because folks don't come in and out of my front door, they come in my side door, so my spike and my broom are behind that door. You need to feed the spike at least once a month with some whiskey and at least burn a tea light cross setup around the spike. It should keep the spike working.

Salt Lamps

Salt lamps can be worked for light and heavy work. It all depends on what you're trying to do. There are two kinds of salt lamps: the electric one, and the hollow lamps where you can set a tea light. Both of the lamps are unique because of the ways you can work with them.

Hide Your Blessings

You'll need an electric salt lamp for this work. Write your petition of all the blessings you want to hide. In other words, hide means protect so troublesome folks won't throw salt on your blessings. Place the petition in the center of a white handkerchief with five finger grass, broom straw to sweep away all the troubles, licorice root, Master of the Woods, and three devil's shoestrings so the enemy will be tied up in their own tricks. Add a pinch of brown sugar to the mix to keep your home sweet.

Roll the handkerchief toward you and tie it in a knot in the center. Hold the knotted hanky up close to your mouth and state your prayers and your petitions. Feed the hanky some whiskey and tobacco smoke. Now set the handkerchief in a setup of seven-day white candles in the shape of a cross. Say your prayer and petition over the candles as you light them, and you light them in the same order that you set them down. Go daily and say your prayer and petition over the hanky as long as the candles are burning.

The next step is to unscrew the bottom of the electric salt lamp and place the hankey inside. Don't replace the lid. Now you are going to place the loaded salt lamp in the center of a candle setup. State your petitions over the work every day as the candles burn. You are basically repeating the same process that you did when you empowered the hanky. This work is a great trick because the work is locked down inside of the salt lamp where no one can see it nor get to it.

Nail Down a Troublesome Target

As we know, salt holds a memory. It's much like candle wax. Whatever you pray over the salt, the salt soaks up. That's what makes these salt lamps so powerful to work. If you have a troublesome person who is always causing confusion and always stirring problems up in the home, or always coming to the home visiting and causing issues, this little work—and I say little work because it's not a whole lot to it—is just what you need. Like I said, salt will hold a prayer, salt will hold a memory. So to do this work, you need a white handkerchief, some lavender, Master of the Woods, calamus root, a photo of the target, three devil's shoestrings, and some alum.

Lay your handkerchief out on the table. Lay the target's photo on top of the handkerchief. Mark three X's across their mouth. Place the alum on top of their photo. Roll the photo up into a small packet, then take that small packet and place it between the devil's shoestrings. Take your red thread and wrap it around the devil's shoestring and the photo that is trapped inside of them three times. Then you're going to tie three knots. On each knot you are going to say your prayer and petition. You are going to tie the knot and say, "In the name of God the Father" on the first knot, "In the name of God the Son" on the second knot, and "in the name of God the Holy Spirit" on the third knot. Lay the packet on the handkerchief and then add each one of your ingredients on top of that. Make sure that you pray over each ingredient before you add it. Once you have all the ingredients on the handkerchief, fold the handkerchief into a handkerchief noodle then tie a tight knot.

Feed the hanky some whiskey and tobacco smoke. Now set the handkerchief in a setup of seven-day white candles in the shape of a cross. Say your prayer and petition over the candles as you light them and light them in the same order that you set them down. Go daily and say your prayer and petition over the hanky as long as the candles are burning.

The next step is to unscrew the bottom of the electric salt lamp and place the hanky inside. Don't replace the lid. Now you are going to place the loaded salt lamp in the center of a candle setup. State your petitions over the work every day as the candles burn. You are basically repeating the same process that you did when you empowered the hanky. This work is a great trick because the work is locked down inside of the salt lamp where no one can see it nor get to it.

Shut Your Mouth

Sometimes we run across folks who just keep running their mouths and don't know how to shut the hell up. For this work, you need

a hollow salt lamp
a medicine bottle

a photo of the target
duct tape
your ingredients

What I like about this work is that by placing the trick in the lamp, whether that be a packet, petition, Conjure hand, bottle, photo, etcetera, you are locking down the work in the salt. Set salt neutralizes, then the person or the aggravating situation will be brought to a standstill. Each time you burn a tea light or a candle in the salt lamp directly on top of the work, you are adding fire, which will keep the work going.

Cover a photo of the enemy with duct tape while telling them to zip their mouth shut. Fold the photo away from you and nail the photo down with a closed safety pin, a needle, or a nail. This will nail your enemy's mouth shut. Place the nailed packet in the medicine bottle with red pepper, a pinch of sulfur, a pinch of gunpowder, dirt from a red ant's nest, some whiskey to feed the work (it just needs a couple of drops), some tobacco, and a little bit of molasses to slow the troublesome person down. Hold the medicine bottle to your mouth and state your prayer and petition in a strong, firm voice, then seal the bottle.

Shake the bottle while stating your petition. When done, place the bottle upside down in the salt lamp. Burn a tea light in the lamp on your work daily. Take the medicine bottle out and shake it daily as you burn a tea light on the work. By working the bottle upside down, you're turning your enemies on their heads. This also causes confusion where they could even just forget about you because they have so much going on. Repeat the process every day by shaking the bottle and burning a tea light on it in the lamp. This work is harsh, but sometimes a heavy hand is needed to pull out all the stops on the bullshit in your life.

Shakers

Shakers are wonderful tools to work with. They can be loaded with just about anything that can be powered. I like working with them in my setup because you can burn the petition and prayers to ash, mix it with the powdered roots and herbs, then every time you go to say your prayers and your petition over your candle setup, you can shake a little bit of the ingredients into the candle. They are also very good to use if you are trying to drop a powder as a trick.

Everyone knows that I'm crazy about roosters. Roosters are very good at protecting and scratching up messes, so the representation of the rooster spirit helps with any kind of work you are doing. If you are having an issue with prosperity or blocked roads, the rooster is the way to go. Roosters are popular nowadays, so you can find the shaker easily. To do the road-opening work as I did in the photo for a client, you need a rooster shaker, five bills of any denomination out of your wallet, twelve tea light candles, and some powdered roots and herbs.

You will need five finger grass, bay leaves, some dried orange peel, and some dirt from the front and back door stoops. You can use a coffee grinder to powder the ingredients, if you need to. Mix all the ingredients together, pray your petition over them, then add them to your shaker. Make sure that before you put the cap on the shaker you pray your prayer and petition into the shaker. Call the spirit of the rooster and ask that rooster to scratch and remove all blocks that are on your money. Lay the money out in the sign of a cross, place the rooster in the center, and then place a tea light candle on each arm of the cross. Call on the Holy Trinity, your ancestors, and the spirit of the rooster to remove all blocks and cross conditions out of your way. Take this shaker out of the center of this setup and sprinkle a little in each one of the tea lights, then put it back in the center. You need to burn this setup for three days in a row. Repeat the same process daily. Once the work is done, sprinkle some of the powder on the soles of your shoes and a little across the front door stoop of your home. Repeat the process as needed.

Shakers can be worked with for many different things. Most folks keep a salt shaker sitting on their kitchen table. This work is all about tricks. It's about being tricky.

There is an old work that tells us that if you sprinkle salt behind someone that you don't want to come back to your home and use the broom to sweep the salt out to the road, then that person won't be back. You could also pick up the salt shaker, walk behind the target all the way out to the road to their vehicle, dropping salt and praying under your breath that they not return to your home. This trick works great also.

Skulls

Skulls are very powerful to work with since they represent the human head. If you have a case that you just can't seem to get finished or if the target just seems to be elusive, then the skull candle is the way to go. A lot of folks don't know how to load these candles or how to burn them so they don't all burn up at one time. The trick to burning a skull candle is to burn them a little bit at a time. This candle should not be wasted and burned all at once. I usually burn them in fifteen-minute intervals. The first step is to get the candle ready. Until the candle is worked and loaded, it's just a ball of wax that looks like a human skull. I know sometimes it's hard to load these candles with roots and herbs. I have found a way that works well for me, so I'm going to share it with you. The best way to make a hole in this type of candle is either with a screwdriver or a small drill. I personally prefer a screwdriver.

The other trick is to load the candle from the top instead of the bottom. Take this screwdriver and press down into the wax. Turn the screwdriver as if you were tightening up a screw. Once you get the hole started, wiggle the screwdriver around in small circles to make the hole larger. Then lightly load your ingredients into the hole. There's no need to get heavy-handed; more is not always better with this type of candle. If you add too many ingredients, it's going to catch on fire, and when you're burning this type of candle, you really need to pay attention and watch it as it burns. There's no need to get heavy-handed because the ingredients are not the only thing that makes the candle work your prayers and your petitions, and also add power to the work, so just take it easy when you're loading these candles up. Also burning them fifteen minutes at a time makes the work stronger. If you let the skull burn all at once, not only have you wasted a skull but you've basically wasted the work. This is one of those works that you cannot rush. You have to take your time doing it if you want your work to be a success.

To Control a Lover

For this work you need

- a photo of the target burnt to ash
- a red skull candle
- calamus root
- Master of the Woods
- dirt dauber's nest
- lovage root
- a small magnet

You need only a pinch of each one of these ingredients; there is no need to overload the skull. Mix all your ingredients together and pray your prayer and petition over them. Load the ingredients into the candle. Hold the candle up to your mouth and call on the Holy Trinity and your ancestors, then call on the name of the target and name the skull candle for the target. Say your prayers and petition over the candle. Let the candle burn for fifteen minutes at a time then snuff the candle out.

During the time that the candle is burning, you need to repeat your prayer and petition over the candle at least three times. Make sure that at the beginning and at the end of your prayer and petition you are calling out the target's name. When you first start this work, it's good to go every hour on the hour and burn the skull for fifteen minutes, at least for the first three days. You can also make a double-action work by placing the skull in a crossroads setup using tea light candles. This will empower your work. I was taught that it's always good to do more than one thing when you are trying to do this type of work.

Sponges

Sponges are very good for protection work. Have you ever seen a sponge in a bowl of water and just watched how that sponge soaked up the water? You can make a wash out of olive leaf, bay leaf, and four tablespoons of table salt. Add the wash in a clear glass bowl. Call on the Holy Trinity and the ancestors. Petition them to add their protective powers to the wash. Get a sponge and repeat your prayers and petitions over the sponge three times. Place the sponge in the bowl of wash and place the bowl up high on top of your refrigerator in the kitchen. Check it regularly to make sure there is still wash in the bowl. This is an easy way to have things that are not good in the house, that keep the house stirred up, moved out of the way. The sponge will soak up all the arguments and any cross conditions that have been thrown at your house. The reason it is put in the kitchen on top of the refrigerator is because the kitchen is the heart of the home. This is where everybody gathers. Make sure that the sponge does not get dry. If it dries out, it's not going to work as well. Repeat the process as needed to ensure your home is well protected. When

you change the wash, make sure you cleanse the sponge out with some cool, running water, then all you have to do is remake your wash and put the sponge back on top of the refrigerator.

There are a few tricks that can be done working with sponges in order to keep salty folks and negative energies out of your home. If there is a lot of arguing in your home, you can make a wash out of bay leaf, calamus root, lovage root, lavender, and angelica root. You need four small sponges and four glass bowls. Add the ingredients to a pot of water and boil the water like you were making a tea. When the water starts to boil, turn the fire off and steep the wash.

Make sure the wash is cool. Take your pointing finger and go in the opposite direction of the clock in a circle in the wash and say, "I call on God the Father, God the Son, and God the Holy Spirit," make all the arguments, all the strife, and all the problems be removed from my home, in the name of God the Father, God the Son, and God the Holy Spirit." Then, using that same finger, pick it up out of the wash then put it back in the wash and go in the way the hands of the clock goes. Call on the Holy Trinity and ask them to draw peace and blessings into your home. Pray they Pslam 23 into the wash. Once this is done, pray over your sponges that they might pick up any arguments, anything that's going on in the house that is breaking the peace, then place them in the bowl.

Pour some of the wash over each of the sponges and then take the sponges and place them in the corner wherever the family gathers. Some folks gather in the living room, some in a den, some folks hang out in their bedrooms, some folks hang out in the kitchen. Wherever your family sits together at, that is where you want to place the sponge in those four corners. Make sure that the sponges stay moist. If they dry out, the work dries out. Repeat the process as needed.

Conjure workers believe in foot track magic. We believe that folks can dress their shoes and walk into your home and drop a trick from the bottom of their shoes. One way to stop this is to place a dressed sponge under the doormat inside and outside of your home. You work the sponge so that it will pick up and draw off anything that anyone may be trying to bring into your home. You can dress the sponge on the outside with uncrossing products or blockbuster products, and you dress the sponge that is on the inside that they will be walking on when they pass over the threshold with protection products. You can also make a wash and dip the sponges in the wash and then put them under the rug. The only problem with this is that a wet sponge is going to make the rug wet. If you powder the sponge, then the possibility of the powder working its way up through the rug and letting the person know that you have products on your rug is a real thing. So the best way to do it is to just dress the sponge lightly, pray your prayers and petitions over the sponge, and then place the sponge under the rug. Simple and easy, but powerful.

If you have someone who lives in your home who is always cutting up, trying to argue, and acting a donkey, you can dress a sponge with peaceful-home products and place it under the chair where they sit or under their side of the bed. It just depends on where they're comfortable at inside the home. This little work will settle them down. Dress the chair or their side of the bed with peaceful-home products and this will also help. If you don't have a recipe for peaceful-home wash, spray, or oil, here is a simple recipe that you can make.

You need basil, angelica root, lavender, Master of the Woods, and some lovage root. You can make a wash out of the ingredients and pray Psalm 23 over it along with your personal prayer asking for peace in your home. Soak the sponge in the wash and then place it either under the target's chair where they sit or on the floor under their side of the bed where they sleep.

Stumps

Stumps are wonderful for enemy work. They are also good for holding things. I have found that the best way to do this kind of work is to place the work in a jar and tie a string around the jar so you can take it out of the stump as needed. The reason I say so you could take it out of the stump as needed is because sometimes when folks feel like they're being worked on, they'll do cleansings and stuff to take the work off, so if you're putting the work in the stump that's when they're being hit. If you take it out of the stump, then they get some relief. I call this the yo-yo effect. Of course, you could just leave the work in there so it could rot right along with the stump. I personally prefer to be able to remove the work if I so choose.

Nowadays you don't hear many folks talk about stump work. This is because unless you live out in the country, you will have no clue how to work with a stump, much less what a stump is, because in the city they grind the stumps down. In the country, most of the time they just let them rot. This type of work is meant to cross a target up and/or hold them down. In order for the tree to become a stump, it has to either be cut down, become rotten, or be struck by lightning. Either way, it makes a powerful tool for a Conjure worker to work with. If you have a rotten stump on your property, all you have to do is make a packet out of the ingredients that you choose and drop it into the stump. As the stump rots, it will do the rest.

Tire Containers

What y'all know 'bout tire planters? Think Conjure! Okay, I'll tell ya! Back in the day, ol' tires were used as planters, not just because they had a use for them, but all ol' Conjure workers know they were a form of protection. My mama had hers painted white. Some were painted red or blue. Tires planted with plants like touch-me-nots were great for unwanted guests. If you had someone that, every time they came to your house, everything just got stirred up and there was always an issue, then you could stop them from coming by putting a work on either side of the door stoop in a tire planter. The reason the tires work so well is what do tires do? They carry a car back and forth to the destination that the driver needs to go into. Therefore they can be worked to pull somebody into the home or to remove somebody away from the home. You don't hardly ever see tires worked with as plant holders anymore. I have them in my yard but I know what they're for. Most of the time they would remove the rim from the tire. My tire planters have the rim on them, which is good because the rim is an extra layer of protection for the home.

If you decide to do this work, you can use just a regular round tire or you can cut it into a designer shape. It's up to you, but they are simple to make. If you're going to use just the round tire then you need to cut something round that can be placed inside the tire so the potting soil will stay in the planter. Like I said, mine are made on the rim, which makes it easier. They simply pulled the tire up to the top of the rim and the rest of the rim became the planter stand. Either way works.

If you have a target that you don't want coming back to your home, you can literally plant them in a tire planter next to the door stoop and stop them from coming to your home. To do this work, you need a nice plant that can live outside, dirt from the four stop signs at a crossroads, a photo of the target, some barberry root, some calamus root, some angelica root, some devil's bit to bind the devil, and you need the foot track from the target, if you can get it. If you can't get it then just leave that part out.

You plant the photo in the planter and you cover it with a little bit of dirt. You call the person's name and you tell them that as long as that plant grows they cannot come back to your home. Then you put each of your herbs and dirt on top of their photo while you say your prayer and petition that this person stop coming to your home because they are causing confusion and upset every time they come. Then you plant your plant on top of all the ingredients. If you do not take care of this work and you let that plant die, then the work is going to die, but as long as you water that plant and you say your prayers and petition over that plant and you take care of it, the work will continue to live. It really is all up to you. If you have a hard time taking care of plants, then get a plant like the iron plant or a cactus, something that is easy to keep alive.

I'm gonna share one more work with you to help draw prosperity into the home. You need a photo of your home, dirt from the four corners of your home, lavender, basil, calamus root, and orange peel. You also need a magnet. You need an ivy plant because the ivy runs and it will go and literally find you prosperity. Put a little potting soil in the pot then add all your ingredients to the pot while you are praying your prayer that prosperity find its way into your home as this ivy grows. Then you plant your plant on top of all the ingredients. Place the planter near the front door of your home. Let the ivy run. Make sure that you take care of this plant and remember that a plant is a living thing. By working this plant, if someone threw at you, the plant would probably give off signs. When someone throws roots at your house and you have plants, spirit can tell the difference between the two living things, and plants are a living thing. So just take care of the plant. Let it grow. Say your prayers and your petitions over it every time you water it. Keep a journal on how your prosperity is going. Just passing on a bit of lost knowledge.

Old Tobacco Tin

You need a tin can, four coins from your pocket, five finger grass, hair from the crown of your head, dirt from the front door stoop of your home, and Master of the Woods. You also need five tea light candles. Lay all your ingredients out on a white handkerchief. Pray over each ingredient as you are placing it on the handkerchief, then you roll the handkerchief toward you while praying your petition. Place the herbs and ingredients into the center of the handkerchief so when you roll it, you will be able to tie the handkerchief into a knot in the center, then place the handkerchief in your can. Then you need to place the can in the candle setup with one tea light sitting on top of the can. Pray your prayers and petitions over the setup as it burns. Once the setup has finished burning, take your tobacco can and place it on your money altar. Make sure to feed it a little whiskey at least once a week and burn a tea light candle on top of it.

Trees

Trees are well known for their Conjure properties. They have been used for a very long time as a protection from the spirit world. Old folks since as long as I can remember have placed blue bottles in trees to keep the spirits away. Trees are also known for healing work. Certain trees are very powerful in this type of work. If you have someone who is ill, wipe them down with a sharp nail. When I say wipe down I don't mean to literally dig the nail into their skin. The nail should never touch their skin. You simply go through the motions as if you were scratching something off. You start from the head to the toe going in the same direction in a downward motion. Cleanse them from the top of their head to the bottom of their feet. Then you need to bring the client to an oak tree. Have the client stand up against the tree, facing you. Place the nail right above their head and hammer the nail into the tree. The tree will pull the illness off of the client, and it won't be long until they should be feeling better.

If you have a child who has nightmares, you can clean them off with the nail. Have them stand with their back to the tree, and mark the height where there shoulders hit. With a new hammer, hammer the nail into the tree where you have marked the base of their shoulders. Once their shoulders grow above the nail, the nightmare should stop. Some folks believe that these are old wives' tales, but these are actually workings.

If you have an enemy who just won't stop and leave you alone, you can bind them in one of the branches of a weeping willow tree and they will stop and leave you alone. The weeping willow is a very powerful tree when it comes to Conjure work. It is said that this tree can make a target weep. The old folks say that not just anyone can work with the weeping willow. If you are not gifted to work with the weeping willow and you try to, you could find yourself weeping for the rest of your life. Some folks say this, too, is just an old wives' tale. Who am I to say that it's real.

U

Umbrellas

Umbrellas can be worked with for protection, just like they protect us from the rain and from storms. If you feel like you are being attacked and you need protection, you can do a cleansing bath. Do a reversal on whatever the situation is that's going on, then take a photo of yourself. Dress the photo with spiritual oil on each of the corners and then right on top of your head. Fold the photo up and place it in a piece of tinfoil with the shiny side of the tinfoil facing outward. Take the packet and place it inside of an old umbrella. Don't open the umbrella up all the way, just open it enough for you to be able to slide the packet down inside, then make sure that you wrap it closed so that it doesn't come open. You can then place the umbrella in a safe place.

If you are going to do a protection mark for your whole house then you need to spiritually cleanse your house. Wash all the doors inside and out, then go outside and take a photo of your home. That is what you are going to work with for protection. You follow the same steps; the only difference is that you are working with a photo of your home.

Vines

Vines are wonderful plants to work with. My favorite vining plant is the ivy. The old folks say that if a person can grow an ivy in their home, then love also grows in that home. Any type of running vine can be used in Conjure work. You can plant your target in the vine to hold them down. You can also work with the vines to tie the target or a situation down. I will usually make a packet and either bury it in an ivy or find some vine growing wild and ask to take a piece of it. Then I'll wrap it around my packet. Since I've already shared a work in the working with burying a packet in a potted plant, I'm going to share a work working with the vines.

Please don't ever just rip a plant up out of the ground. Always remember to be respectful, as it is a living thing. Once you have your packet ready, you then need to find a vine that is growing wild. Do not use scissors to cut the vine; remember scissors are worked with in Conjure to cut and remove. They cut the magic. Give the plant a cool drink of water and ask permission to take a small piece of the vine. Once permission is given, break off a couple of feet of the running vine. Take the vine and wrap it around your packet. The direction you wrap in all depends on the type of work you are doing. If you are trying to bring something to you, then you wrap the vine toward you. If you are trying to move something away from you, then you wrap away from you. Once you have the packet wrapped, set it in a candle setup.

You work this packet just like you would any other packet. As the vine dries, it's going to get tighter around the packet.

Vegetables

Vegetables have been worked with for a long time to do many things. They can draw love, they can rock someone's life, they can draw in prosperity. Sweet potato can be worked with to draw prosperity into the home. You need some type of container. An old Mason jar works good, and you need a sweet potato and three nails. First, I'm gonna explain to you what the sweet potato does and then I'll explain how to put it together. Once you get the potato and you get it in the water, it's going to root and then potato vines are gonna start growing out of it. As those potato vines grow, your money is going to start growing, and I'm gonna tell you how after I tell you how to fix the potato.

You need three flat-head nails, your potato, and the old jar that you are going to put the potato in. You need quarter, a nickel, and a dime out of your wallet. Place the coins in the jar and put water in the jar, but don't fill it all the way to the top. Take the three nails and place

them in the potato in the shape of a triangle. This is what is going to hold the potato up out of the water. Once you get that done, set the potato in the jar. Make sure that the potato is not touching the water, because if it does, it's gonna rot the potato. Set the jar somewhere in a window where it can get light. Every day, go talk to that plant, and I say plant because it is literally gonna turn into a plant. Before long you will see a vine is starting to grow out of the top of that potato.

Once the vines get long enough, you can take small pieces of paper and write your petition on that paper. Wrap it on the stem, and as the plant grows, whatever you are asking for should come to fruition. You have to remember that this is a living thing, so therefore you have to take care of it. You have to make sure that it has enough water, and you have to make sure that it does not become root-bound in the jar. If it does happen to become root-bound, then you simply gently move it into a larger jar. As long as you take care of the plant it will take care of you.

Wax Doll

Wax dolls are one of my favorite dolls to work with. You can either make them out of a soft wax that you get at the candle supply shop or you can make them out of beeswax. This type of dollie is a freeform dollie. Soft wax is the easiest way to make this type of doll because it is easier to shape into a gingerbread shape. All your ingredients can be added right into the wax as you are forming the doll. I prefer to focus on the head of the doll. This is where I tend to add my ingredients; after all, our heads rule our hearts.

Self-Love Dollie

There are so many folks nowadays who don't love themselves. It is very important that we love ourselves like no one else can, if we want to be successful and to have a happy life. You can't depend on someone else for your happiness, because when we do that we are only setting ourselves up to be hurt and to try to meet expectations that we can never meet. We have to love ourselves first. We have to understand ourselves. We cannot put ourselves in somebody else's hands to make us happy and to make us feel loved. All of that starts inside of us. We all go through things in our lives that could destroy us if we let them, but self-love has to be at the very top of the things that are important to us. When we love ourselves and we have high self-esteem, and we find somebody that loves us for who we are, that's a bonus, because when you love yourself, you don't need anybody else to validate you. This may be the most important work in this whole book.

For this doll, you need lovage root, Master of the Woods, Solomon's seal root, and the hair from the crown of your head. Form the doll from a piece of soft wax. While you are making the form of your doll, make sure that you are praying your prayer and your petition over the wax. Petition as you make the dollie that all things that have hurt you and made you feel less of yourself be removed, and that this wax doll be filled with self-love and self-appreciation. Once you have the doll made, take your finger and make a hole in the crown of the doll's head, then pack your ingredients into the doll's head and cover it with a little extra wax. Then make a little hole where the doll's heart would be. Place a little bit of lovage root into the hole and cover it up with a small piece of wax.

Once you have the doll made and loaded, place it in a triangle setup. For this setup, work with seven-day white candles. Place the first candle at the top, the second candle to the left, and the third candle to the right. You're going left to right because we want to lock this feeling of love down within us. We want it to stick. You need to talk to your dollie, not about how you feel, but how you wanna feel. You don't wanna put what you feel like right now into that doll, you wanna put your hopes and dreams into that doll. After the candles burn out, wrap your doll in a white handkerchief. Place the doll in a safe place because this doll represents you. You do not want someone getting that doll. The best way for success with this type of doll is to work the doll daily. There is no great hocus-pocus to this. You just talk to the doll, tell the doll how you love yourself, how you love life, how you enjoy being alive. It takes ninety days to change a thought. Just keep working your doll and keep it safe.

Whiskey Flask

A whiskey flask is a great tool when you need offerings on the go, but then you may just need it for a job. You can do a work in a whiskey flask and take the flask with you so you will have the work with you at all times if it is an ongoing work. You can also add whiskey to the work and it won't leak out. By adding whiskey to the work you are not only feeding the work but you are also heating up the work. These small flasks are also good when you are trying to move someone away from you on the job. Here's how to do it.

You need the name or photo of the target, calamus root, Master of the Woods, one dried red pepper, and the dirt from a crossroads moving away from your job. Load everything into the flask while praying your petition that the target leave the job and move on to a better, paying job. Feed the ingredients some whiskey, close the flask, and work it in a candle setup. When the flask is ready, you take it to work with you so it will be close to the target. Shake the flask up and pray your petition all through the day that the target be moved out and find a better-paying job. Soon the target will move along because they have found a better-paying job. This is not a hotfoot work because you are not running the target off the job. You are helping them find a job that pays more and suits them better, where they may be able to get along with folks.

CLOSING

First, I would like to say thank you for your support and the purchase of this book. This book is filled with a lot of useful information that can help you achieve the goals without breaking the bank. The works in this book are all works that I have either been taught by my elders or they are my own works. I shared a few that I have shared before because I feel like they are important works that work well, and that they would be useful in this book of container works. There is also a lot of work in this book that I have never shared before.

I enjoyed writing this book and I'm sure that I could have added a lot more to the book, because there are no limitations to the works that can be done using containers. These works are very important because the more you pray your prayers and you burn on your work, the more power the work is going to build within the container. I personally prefer to work with containers. For me, they seem to work well. Just remember that in order for work to continue to work, you have to be diligent and do the work or you will just be wasting your time. I want to leave you with this: Remember that you and only you are responsible for the works that you do. It is not the writer, it is not the target, it is you. Always remember every action causes a reaction and any work that has been done can be reversed. Justice is the key-word when you are doing this type of work. If you do divination and spirit tells you that the work is unjustified and not to do it, then don't do the work. Just let it go because spirit is going to take care of the situation themselves. If you follow this one rule you will save yourself a lot of heartache and a lot of trouble. Always divine on the situation before you lift a finger to do any type of magical workings.

Be blessed and I hope that you enjoyed reading this book.

ABOUT THE AUTHOR

Starr Casas was born in the mountains of Kentucky and raised in the culture of the Deep South, and she continues to hold tight to the folkways of her ancestors. At the age of seventeen, Starr learned how to do cleansings with eggs, herbs, and candles. She has been a Conjure woman for over forty years and she is the fourth generation of her family to practice traditional Southern Conjure. A beloved teacher, she presents workshops across the United States. She lives in Texas, outside of Houston. Find her at *oldstyleconjure.com* or follow her on Instagram at @starrcasas.

To Our Readers

Weiser Books, an imprint of Red Wheel/Weiser, publishes books across the entire spectrum of occult, esoteric, speculative, and New Age subjects. Our mission is to publish quality books that will make a difference in people's lives without advocating any one particular path or field of study. We value the integrity, originality, and depth of knowledge of our authors.

Our readers are our most important resource, and we appreciate your input, suggestions, and ideas about what you would like to see published.

Visit our website at *www.redwheelweiser.com*, where you can learn about our upcoming books and free downloads, and also find links to sign up for our newsletter and exclusive offers.

You can also contact us at *info@rwwbooks.com* or at

Red Wheel/Weiser, LLC
65 Parker Street, Suite 7
Newburyport, MA 01950